Practical
Self-Defense

Practical
Self-Defense

Mike Lorden

Tuttle Publishing

Boston ■ Rutland, VT ■ Tokyo

The author and publisher do not claim that you can become a self-defense expert by studying the contents of this book alone. We do not imply that you will become a self-defense expert in a matter of weeks or suggest that you will be able to apply these techniques after only a few lessons. It is strongly recommended that you seek out and undertake a continuous training regime with a legitimate and certified martial art or self-defense instructor. Please note that the author and publisher are NOT RESPONSIBLE in any manner whatsoever for any injury that may result from practicing the techniques and/or following the instructions given within. The physical activities described herein may be too strenuous in nature for some readers to engage in safely. Injuries can occur in martial arts and self-defense training, and because of this it is strongly recommended that you receive a medical clearance from a doctor before you begin.

First published in 2003 by Tuttle Publishing, an imprint of Periplus Editions (HK) Ltd., with editorial offices at 153 Milk Street, Boston Massachusetts 02109.

Library of Congress Cataloging-in-Publication Data
Lorden, Mike, 1951-
    Practical self-defense / Mike Lorden.—1st ed.
    p. cm.
    ISBN 0-8048-3446-6
    1. Self-defense. 2. Karate. I. Title

GV1111 .L68 2003
613.6'6—dc21   2002075656

Distributed by

North America, Latin America, and Europe
Tuttle Publishing
Distribution Center
Airport Industrial Park
364 Innovation Drive
North Clarendon, VT 05759-9436
Tel: (802) 773-8930
Fax: (802) 773-6993
Email: info@tuttlepublishing.com

Japan
Tuttle Publishing
Yaekari Bldg., 3F
5-4-12 Ōsaki, Shinagawa-ku
Tokyo 141-0032
Tel: 81-35-437-0171
Fax: 81-35-437-0755
Email: tuttle-sales@gol.com

Asia Pacific
Berkeley Books Pte. Ltd.
130 Joo Seng Road
#06-01/03 Olivine Building
Singapore 368357
Tel: (65) 6280-3320
Fax: (65) 6280-6290
Email: inquiries@periplus.com.sg

First edition
08 07 06 05 04 03 9 8 7 6 5 4 3 2 1

Design by Stephanie Doyle
Printed in Canada

"The credit belongs to the man who is actually in the arena, whose face is marred by dust and sweat and blood . . . who knows the great enthusiasm, the great devotions; who spends himself at a worthy cause; who at best knows in the end the triumph of high achievement, and . . . if he fails, at least fails daring greatly so that his place shall never be with those cold, timid souls who know neither victory nor defeat."

John Fitzgerald Kennedy

This book is dedicated to the men and women of law enforcement who put their lives on the line everyday for the safety of others.

Contents

Acknowledgments

This book would not have been possible if not for the support, insight, and guidance from my wife, Jennifer. I am also greatly indebted to the following friends and colleagues for their support and unstinting help in the preparation of this book: Eugene Chavez (photographer), Jonn Lee Alinsunurin, and Danny Fuller.

Introduction

Practical Self-Defense is a guide, a reference, and a resource, but on a more personal level, it is also an aide to building confidence and establishing day-to-day safety awareness and tactics for personal protection.

This book will take you on a journey, pointing out options and helping you make decisions about safety procedures and personal protection in your life. It will teach you how to view your surroundings for possible danger and threats. It will also help you understand your mental and physical limitations and capabilities. This personal recognition is the first and most important aspect of self-defense. After you have an understanding of your limitations and capabilities you will be able to learn how to minimize these limitations and enhance your capabilities.

The techniques shown in this book are not foolproof, just as life is not foolproof. The book provides insights and responses that are applicable for daily life, and it will guide you through the complexities of personal crime, from which no one is immune. There are hundreds of books that deal with karate and self-defense. These books show sequential photographs of self-defense scenarios. None of them, however, deal with the specifics of crime, precautions, awareness, confidence building, anatomy and physiology, physical conditioning, home and travel safety, and applicable personal protection tactics. *Practical Self-Defense* is unique in that it allows the reader to glance at the Table of Contents and locate the chapter that deals with a specific issue. No other book on self-defense and personal protection offers this.

The many elements of self-defense are described and explained. Although it is impossible to do justice to such a complex concept, the information contained herein will provide a solid basis for a firm understanding of practical self-defense.

1

The Way of Self-Defense

Insight

One who knows the enemy and knows himself will not be endangered in a hundred engagements. One who does not know the enemy but knows himself will sometimes be victorious, sometimes meet with defeat. One who knows neither the enemy nor himself will invariably be defeated in every engagement.

Sun-Tzu

The above passage, from Sun-Tsu's classic, *The Art of War*, cannot be more applicable than to the practice of self-defense. Knowing yourself and your opponent is paramount to success. If you are unaware or unsure of your physical or mental capabilities and limitations, you will not be successful in a personal-protection encounter. The only way to know yourself is with proper and thorough self-defense training.

In the eyes of the law, *reasonably necessary* is the key factor for anyone involved in a self-defense situation. This means that you are *only* allowed to use minimum force to defend yourself or others. Escalation of force is authorized only if there is an increased level of violence or bodily harm to the defender. If you go beyond what is reasonably necessary in the defense of others or yourself, you could be charged with a crime or sued by the attacker.

In my karate classes and in the various self-defense programs I instruct, I tell my students, "You learn to fight in order to avoid the fight." Proper training in a valid martial art or self-defense program not only teaches you to be aware of your physical and mental limitations, but also to be aware of your surroundings. Both of these skills will help you avoid locales, leisure activities, and situations where confrontations are predictable. There is a saying, "If you choose to run away, you live to fight another day." Confrontations should be avoided at all costs. If you exhaust all avenues of remedy, however, and you are faced with a situation requiring self-defense, use only the force that is reasonably necessary.

It is probably accurate to say that most people who begin training in a martial art do so for the purpose of self-defense. This may be due to a violent incident they experienced or read about, or they may just want to be better prepared to protect themselves and their family. It is not uncommon for new students who are just beginning to learn the basic stances and techniques to inquire when the self-defense training will start. Many novice (and some not-so-novice) students believe that martial arts and self-defense training is only about learning how to kick, punch, escape holds, and block or stop an attack. However, the moment a student begins training in the karate *dojo* (training hall) he or she is learning self-defense, and much of it is not about kicks and punches. Every aspect of a student's training has self-defense applications. All of the following elements of karate play a critical role in self defense.

- *Kihon*—the basic techniques of blocking, kicking, striking, and punching.
- *Kata*—the pre-arranged forms of movement combining defense and counter.
- *Renraku*—the transitional training using various combinations of blocks and counters.
- *Sanbon-kumite* and *Ippon-kumite*—pre-arranged fighting with a partner.
- *Jiyu-kumite*—free-fighting with an opponent.
- *Ibuki* and *Nogare*—required proper breathing methods.
- *Meditation*—often overlooked when it comes to practical application, this plays a significant role in self-defense.
- *Taiso*—physical conditioning, another important aspect of self-defense that is not only overlooked, but is excluded in many training regimens.

The techniques displayed in this book are primarily drawn from the martial art of karate, more specifically Kyokushin Karate. Kyokushin emphasizes physical conditioning and the need for cross training in weight resistance and aerobic activities. From its beginnings in the early '50s, Kyokushin instructors have stressed the use of full contact during training. Kyokushin is the originator of training without protective equipment. The innovative way of full-contact training not only teaches the student the proper method of muscular tension when executing blocks, it also brings an awareness of the power and pain experienced when strikes make contact with the body. Full-contact training increases in levels of intensity as the student progresses from novice to more experienced and is carefully monitored by the instructor.

Although a strong emphasis is placed on physical conditioning and full-contact training, these are only two of a myriad of elements that comprise the extensive training regimen of Kyokushin Karate. The training is intense and demanding, both physically and mentally. The versatile subject matter makes it most applicable for real-life self-defense.

In Kyokushin Karate, there is a saying, *ko-gaku-shin*, or maintain an open mind to learn. In my Kyokushin school, the emphasis, as you will gather from this book, is on self-defense. There are no trophies nor a sporting atmosphere of one-up-man-ship. The goal is total well-being, which includes self-protection. Every aspect of training, including the seemingly mundane and insignificant, serves a purpose toward achieving that goal. This is why it is most important for the student to maintain an open mind to learning.

There is a lot to learn and absorb, and students realize quickly that the key to advancement is hard work with plenty of sweat, patience, and diligence. Because of this, students are encouraged to attend class as often as possible, even if they are restricted from physical involvement and can only watch. If a student has a physical difficulty, other than a cold or flu that prohibits participation in the physical phase of training, I recommend still attending class.

Observation is an important aspect of training. It is difficult, however, for a student to sit and watch a class, not taking part in the physical aspect of training. In this situation, the student does not have to contend with the endurance, the muscle fatigue and soreness, and all the other agonizing elements associated with physical exercise. This freedom from physical discomfort can allow the mind to focus its attention on observation. This, in turn, will allow the student to analyze and digest the instructions and information he or she may have heard over and over again.

Less experienced students generally want to learn as many techniques as they can, as fast as they can. They see a myriad of techniques performed by the senior students. Right away, novice students want to perform these techniques. They are not satisfied with their own repertoire; they feel that more is better, and that more techniques must be the key to promotion to the next belt level. At this point, their minds are closed to learning. They are focused on quantity, because surely, quantity must be the fast track to promotion. They ask the seniors to teach them the new techniques, not understanding that this is not one of the senior student's duties. The senior student is there to guide and nurture the junior student, not to provide shortcuts. There are no shortcuts in martial arts, just as there are no shortcuts in life.

Like the eager, less-experienced students, many in society today believe the emphasis should be on quantity, rather than quality. They believe that knowing a little something about a multitude of things is the fast track to advancement. They do not want to acknowledge that anything done in haste and lacking quality is doomed for failure. (The recent collapse of several major corporations is proof in this belief that quantity, even if deceitfully inflated, is more important than quality.) They too, like the eager martial art students, closed their minds to learning.

Proficiency in martial arts, self-defense, and life requires one to maintain an open mind to learn, ko-gaku-shin.

2

Self-Defense and Survival

According to Federal Bureau of Investigation (FBI) statistics, one violent crime occurs every twenty seconds in the United States. The statistics also show that there are approximately 8.3 million violent attacks against persons twelve years and older every year, or thirty-nine victims per one thousand residents in the U.S. in this age bracket. An estimated five out of six people will be victims of either completed or attempted violent crimes once in their lives (Koppel, 1987). Overall, violent crimes were committed against men thirty percent more often than against women. However, women suffered rape or sexual assault at a rate of fifteen times greater than men. According to the National Women's Study, 683,000 forcible rapes occur every year, which equals 56, 916 per month; 1,871 per day; 78 per hour, and 1.3 per minute.

The cost of crime in the U.S. is staggering. David Anderson of Centre College reports in the *Journal of Law and Economics* that crime in the U.S. is at a cost of *1.7 trillion dollars per year.*

What is self-defense? *Webster's Dictionary* defines self-defense as: "(1) defense of oneself or of one's rights, beliefs, actions, etc. (2) the right to defend oneself with whatever force is reasonably necessary against actual or threatened violence."

In order to defend yourself against violence you must possess the ability to do so. This ability can only be achieved through training. A new military recruit would not be expected to go into combat and survive. Why would anyone without defensive-skills training believe they could survive an act of violence? Without adequate training it is highly unlikely.

You cannot assume that surrendering money or possessions to an assailant will assure your safety. You cannot know the full intent or mental state of the individual who is assaulting you. Life-threatening situations place both the assailant and the victim under a tremendous amount of stress, and numerous physical and mental factors come into play. Thoughts and actions can become irrational. This holds true whether the assault is real or threatened.

Personal protection is the ability to successfully safeguard yourself and your family from acts of violence. Adequate personal protection requires developing a survival attitude, which means that you must be willing to defend against an assailant with exceptional determination using all resources available. If you are not prepared to go *all out* you may become the next fatality on a long list of statistics.

Many people are under the notion that *it* (crime) will not happen to them. All you have to do is look at the statistics to see that this is not true. Shooting rampages, home invasions, and car-jackings were unheard of until a few years ago. It is a sad reflection on humanity that today everyone is familiar with them. Is there anything that you can do to prevent becoming a victim of any of these horrendous acts of violence? Yes!

Most people go about their day-to-day activities oblivious to their surroundings. If you do not believe this is so, just step back and watch people as they drive a vehicle or talk on a cell-phone. In addition, most people are not even aware of the actions that make them vulnerable to a criminal attack. Again, step back and watch. See the woman bagging her groceries at the checkout counter, while her purse lies open several feet away? Or how about the woman who is at one end of the grocery store isle, while her cart, containing her purse is at the opposite end of the isle? Then there is the man who pulls up in front of the convenience store, rushes from his vehicle into the store, leaving his vehicle running and unattended. We have all read or heard of the individuals who claim they forgot that they left their child in a closed-up vehicle, baking under the sun, while they went shopping, or to work, or some other activity for several hours. What happened to that little thing called common sense—and what does it have to do with self-defense?

When I ask individuals to define self-defense, their answers are similar. In some form or another, all their responses allude to the use of physical force for protection. No one ever mentions the mental aspect of self-defense, which involves the use of our senses: sight, hearing, smell, taste, and touch. Our senses should act as radars, scanning our surroundings and the activities taking place around us. Being aware will allow you to avoid the vicinities and conditions that pose a danger of physical harm. An even greater role in the mental aspect, however, is awareness of your actions. You do not want your actions to place you in a position of vulnerability or endanger others, as did the individuals mentioned at the beginning of this section. People who are oblivious of their own actions are not employing the most important sense of all—common sense. The following helpful reminders are based on common sense.

Safety Tips

WHILE TRAVELING IN A VEHICLE

- To prevent becoming stranded, maintain a mechanically sound vehicle at all times.
- To prevent unwanted mishaps and incidents, perform a visual check of your vehicle before entering. Look for the following: tag, door or trunk tampering, broken windows, deflated tires, obstacles near vehicle.
- Look inside your vehicle (front and rear) before entering to be sure no one is lurking inside.
- Keep all the doors locked when you are traveling. This is the first step toward preventing a car-jacking or robbery as you sit waiting for the red traffic light to change.
- Wear your seat belt at all times.
- Keep your car windows closed whenever possible (using the air conditioning with windows up will use less gas).

- If you are approached and feel threatened, use the car horn and lights as an alarm to attract attention. Flee the area immediately.
- If you are being flagged down by a car flashing blue lights, but you are suspicious of the validity of its law enforcement credentials, continue to drive slowly and safely to a public area, police station, or fire department. If it is a law enforcement officer explain your concerns and actions. Many people have been attacked after stopping their vehicles for fictitious emergency vehicles.
- Be familiar with the area in which you are traveling and know an alternate route to your planned destination.
- Travel with a companion whenever possible, especially on long or unfamiliar routes.
- Carry a flashlight and flares in your vehicle in case your vehicle breaks down or you find yourself in a situation that requires these items.
- Carry a spare vehicle key in the event you lock your keys inside your car.
- If stranded in a remote area because of mechanical failure, stay with your vehicle. This is especially important if you are in poor health or physical condition, and if you are not prepared for the weather. Tie something white (a handkerchief, clothing) on the antenna or on the highest point of the vehicle. This is a sign indicating assistance is needed.
- Be aware of the occupants in the vehicles around you.
- Be aware of vehicles that continue to follow you.
- Keep vehicle and house keys in separate areas.
- Before approaching your vehicle, have the key in your hand and ready.
- If you believe you are being followed, drive to the nearest law enforcement office, fire station, or public area.
- If you are walking to your vehicle and believe you are being followed, *do not* go to your vehicle. Continue to a populated area and summon help.
- When stopping behind another vehicle, leave enough room to see the tires of the vehicle in front of you. This allows enough room to pull out of the line of traffic, not only in situations where you are threatened, but also when yielding the right of way to emergency vehicles.
- If your vehicle has a standard transmission and you are stopped at a traffic light or a stop sign, maintain the vehicle in gear rather than in neutral.
- Back in to parking places whenever possible to allow for a quick get away.
- Never leave your keys in the ignition when pumping gas at a service station. If your vehicle is stolen, it is possible you could receive a summons.
- Never leave your car running while unattended. This is a traffic infraction in most areas. This is especially true if you leave children in the vehicle. Eight children were abducted throughout the country between March and August, 2002. Only three of the children were recovered.
- Do not place any stickers on your vehicle advertising where you live or work. This may be difficult if your place of residence or work requires such a sticker. Most places that require an ID sticker are starting to see the error in this,

and are beginning to issue coded stickers that do not indicate the establishment. If your sticker identifies an establishment, attempt to conceal it whenever possible.

■ Maintain the following in your vehicle in case your car breaks down:

1. First-aid kit
2. Fire extinguisher, spare water, and oil
3. Inclement weather attire
4. Tools, spare fuses, belts, etc.
5. Cellular phone (if traveling alone)
6. Spare key in a magnetic box attached under the frame

TRAVELING ON FOOT

■ Beware of your surroundings at all times. This reduces the risk of entering a dangerous situation.

■ Walk with confidence; do not look scared or unsure. It is a known fact that criminals target people who look like victims.

■ Accept the probability of becoming a victim and learn to recognize and avoid potentially dangerous situations.

■ Try to avoid danger areas: alleys, deserted lots, and poorly lit, undesirable neighborhoods.

■ Travel with others whenever possible. It is true that there is safety in numbers.

■ If you carry a purse, suspend it diagonally across your body and hold it under your arm. If you can, wear your purse under your coat. This discourages thieves who snatch and run.

■ Carry money in your front pants pocket, or inside the pockets of your shirt, jacket, or sweater. Do not carry money in your wallet. Criminals do their homework more than you can imagine. They know most people carry their money in a wallet. It is not an inconvenience to carry your money in a pocket.

■ Do not lay your wallet or purse on the counter at a store when you pay for your merchandise.

■ Request receipts and carbon copies of credit card purchases from merchants. This prevents others from obtaining your credit card information and making unauthorized purchases.

■ Memorize personal identification numbers (PINs) for accounts and credit cards. Do not write them down on anything.

■ Remain alert whenever using an automatic teller machine. They are prime locations for robberies and purse snatchings.

■ Carry a whistle, preferably around your neck, and use it if needed. It is a fact that individuals will respond to the sound of a whistle more readily than a cry for help. In addition, the sound startles, and can confuse an assailant.

■ If you are in a situation and need to summon help, scream, "Fire." More people are apt to respond to a cry of "Fire," than to a cry for help.

- Know your physical limitations. Practice a martial art or other fighting skill, if for nothing more than to understand your limitations and develop reactionary skills.
- When trying on clothes in stores, do not leave your valuables unattended.
- Maintain control of your valuables when you use a restroom.
- If you carry a defensive device (mace, pepper-spray, stun-gun, or firearm), become familiar with its applications and effectiveness, as well as with the legal issues surrounding its use. Keep it near you when traveling. None of these items are helpful if you cannot get to them in a hurry, and when under stress. An attacker is not going to allow time for you to rummage through a purse, backpack, or even the pockets of your clothing to retrieve your weapon.
- When using a telephone calling card, conceal the numbers from others.
- When using an elevator, stay close to the control panel. If you are attacked in an elevator, press as many floor buttons as possible. Do not try to locate the alarm button. Do not hit the stop button.

At Home

- Own a dog (or a recording device of a dog set on a timer).
- Invest in an alarm system (pressure, vibration, motion, microwave, seismic, or others).
- Maintain adequate insurance coverage.
- Install outdoor lighting, controlled by photocell or timer.
- Periodically change the hours on your timers.
- If you keep a firearm in your home, become proficient with its nomenclature and operation, and keep it securely away from any children.
- Install dead-bolt locks on your doors. Electronic locks should have battery back-up and secondary locks.
- Install supplemental locking devices on *all* windows.
- Install a device (peep-hole, closed circuit television) for outside viewing of entrance areas.
- Use an answering machine and caller ID to screen telephone calls.
- Obtain a confidential telephone listing. If you must list your number, use your first initial only, and never use Mr., Ms., or Mrs.
- Educate your children on proper telephone answering procedures.
- Maintain a list of all emergency numbers near the telephone. If possible, program them into autodial.
- If you are alone at home and someone arrives, call out to verify who is there before opening the door.
- Avoid sleeping with your windows open.
- Trim high plants and foliage that conceal your doors and windows.
- If you live alone, add fictional names to your mailbox, and at the post office. Make it appear that others live with you.

- Secure your garage door openers when you are away, including the security codes.
- Leave the television or radio on when you are not at home, or put them on timers.
- Keep your curtains and blinds closed at night. It is difficult to see out, but easy to see in.
- Do not close all curtains and blinds when you are away from home. This looks out of place and inviting to criminals.
- Photograph and/or video all valuables. Engrave them if possible.
- Maintain your house keys separate from your vehicle keys.
- When approaching your residence, have your key out and ready.
- Establish an emergency alert signal with your neighbors.
- Know the location of circuit breakers and utility mains to the house. If they are located outside, cover and secure them with a locking device.
- Do not place any stickers on your vehicle that advertise where you live. See the accompanying information to this tip above, under the heading: While Traveling in a Vehicle.
- Install a dual lighting system and have a battery back up.
- Install a fence around the perimeter of your property.
- Install shatter-resistant film on your windows.
- Have your communication and power lines buried.
- Maintain the following:

  1. Smoke alarms
  2. Fire extinguishers
  3. Flashlights
  4. Extra batteries
  5. Bottled water
  6. First aid kit

AT WORK

- Do not assume that because you work inside (office, hospital, or warehouse) you are free from danger.
- Do not take any threat lightly.
- Pay attention to the body language of others.
- Avoid potential danger areas.
- Do not leave valuables unsecured.
- Familiarize yourself with the layout of the building.
- Know the locations of emergency exits, fire alarms, and fire extinguishers.
- Maintain a list of emergency telephone numbers.
- If you need to work late advise someone, especially if you will be alone.
- If possible, park your vehicle in a well-lit area.
- Remain alert when traveling to and from your vehicle.
- In the event of a fire do not use an elevator.

CHILDREN

- Educate your children about possible dangers.
- Secure any firearms that you maintain in your home.
- If small children are present cover all unused electrical outlets.
- Secure all household items that could cause injury or harm.
- Educate children on proper telephone answering procedures:
    1. If they are very young, restrict them from answering the telephone.
    2. If they do answer, they should never tell anyone that they are alone. Although it is necessary for parents who work to leave children home alone, it is unadvisable, especially for children under the age of fourteen. If you must leave your children alone maintain a system where they contact you at pre-arranged times. In addition, ask a trusted neighbor, and if possible a second as a backup, to check on your children on a regular basis during your absence.
    3. They should never tell the caller who else is home.
    4. Test them periodically on emergency numbers.
    5. Do not allow them to use a re-dial system.

- Emphasize the dangers of allowing strangers to approach them.
- Teach them to walk against the traffic when they are on foot.
- If approached by a stranger in a vehicle, instruct them to run in the opposite direction that the vehicle is facing.
- Advise them not to listen to a stranger's offer of candy, money, or plea for help. (For example, they might have a sick kitten they want the child to come see.)
- Advise them to scream, "Fire" if they need help.
- Help them memorize the names and telephone numbers of parents' friends, their friends, and parents' work.
- Advise them to call if they are going to be late or they have changed their plans.
- *Do not* allow them to open the residence door without identifying the visitor.
- If they are home alone, they should never open the door for anyone except family members.

Personal safety is a matter of education and common sense. The more you learn about yourself, your surroundings, and those around you, the better prepared you will be in the event of an emergency.

We live in a society of uncertainties. Unfortunately many of these uncertainties come in the form of emergencies and criminal actions. While you must be aware of the probabilities of danger, you cannot live in paranoia. We must have the confidence to travel anywhere at anytime, to associate with family and friends, and enjoy life. Anything less and we are no longer free.

3

Stress, Breathing, and Pain

Stress, breathing, and pain are three physiological functions that are vital for a successful outcome to a life-threatening struggle. Understanding the effects of these three functions and the role they play in self-defense is crucial.

Stress

During a life-threatening situation, you are placed under a tremendous amount of stress. Thoughts and actions can become irrational. This holds true whether the situation is real, or perceived to be real. The instant the body is faced with a life-threatening situation (real or perceived) the brain senses the stress and notifies the entire nervous system. In turn, the nervous system triggers behavioral, emotional, and physiological components to respond.

1. Change in behavior
    a. irritability
    b. inappropriate reactions
    c. inability to make decisions

2. Change in emotional responses
    a. panic
    b. fear
    c. anxiety
    d. rage
    e. loss of control

3. Physiological reactions
    a. accelerated breathing
    b. profuse perspiration
    c. rapid heart rate
    d. increased muscle tension
    e. impaired vision

Among these responses to threat and stress are several conditioned responses that, with proper training can bring a favorable outcome. When you are suddenly threatened, *the fight-or-flight syndrome* occurs, which is what determines how you will react to the confrontation. To stand and defend yourself requires ability and confidence. Both of these traits, acquired through comprehensive training, can assure the necessary capacity for an adequate response.

Another response is *panic*. When faced with a life-threatening scenario most individuals will panic, and this is the leading reason that individuals become victims and succumb to the situation confronting them. Most individuals panic because they lack the skill, discipline, confidence, and the means to react to the situation at hand. Panic is the only recourse when you have nothing on which to revert.

An important response to self-defense situations, as well as any situation that requires split-second reaction, is the *dominant response*. The dominant response is the body's reflex response to life-threatening situations, and it can have a positive effect on the fight-or-flight syndrome and panic. Quite simply, your dominant response is how you will react when facing danger. An individual with no skill or confidence will react with panic. People who train in the various fighting arts will, under stress, react according to the way they train. *The way you train is the way you will react.* If your training is not thorough or it is slow and sloppy, the same will be true in a self-defense situation. Your survival mode reaction will be ineffective.

The following is a true account of the way training is carried into survival-mode reactions. A police officer engaged a criminal assailant in a shoot-out. During the course of the shoot-out, the officer's gun emptied of bullets, he reloaded, and again engaged the suspect. The officer was then shot and killed by the suspect. The investigation that followed determined that the officer, after firing all his rounds, opened his weapon, removed the spent cartridges and placed them in his pants pocket. The officer then reached back into his pants pocket for cartridges and reloaded. He again engaged the suspect and that was when he was shot and killed. The investigation concluded that the officer did not reload with fresh rounds, but with the same spent cartridges he placed in his pocket. Further investigation revealed that when the officer practiced on the firing range, not under stress, he placed his spent rounds in his pocket instead of dumping them on the ground, as instructed. He did this to avoid having to pick up the cartridges when he finished his practice. Under stress, the officer simply performed the same way he had trained, only the consequences were fatal.

Your physical health can also affect your dominant response. Life threatening circumstances place your body under an extreme amount of stress. What could be more stressful than fighting for your life or the life of a family member? As mentioned, you can experience several physiological reactions when stress is induced. Blurred vision, tunnel vision, profuse sweating, slurred speech, and diminished thought processing are a few of these stress-induced reactions. Individuals who are in excellent physical condition are not immune from these stress-induced reactions. Their ability to cope and control them, however, will be far greater than that of individuals who are in poor to mediocre physical condition. Physical conditioning also allows you to recognize your physical and mental limitations. If you are not aware of your physical and mental limitations, the outcome in a self-defense encounter could be devastating, and even fatal.

Physical conditioning also helps establish confidence. Individuals who exercise on a regular basis and maintain a high level of physical condition feel good about themselves. They like the way they feel and look. They have a manner of confidence about them when they move. Members of elite military units, like Navy SEALs (Sea-Air-and-Land—U.S.

Navy Special Operation Forces) and Army Special Forces are the epitome of confidence. This is due to the intense and comprehensive nature of their unending cross training.

Breathing

Cross training in physical conditioning exercises, such as weight resistance, and aerobic activities, such as biking, running, and swimming, is necessary in order to enhance the overall condition of your body. Cardiovascular endurance (stamina) and aerobic activities are essential for developing adequate breath control.

Proper breathing is essential for the successful execution of any activity. What constitutes proper breathing? We breathe ten to twelve times per minute, and each breath consists of approximately one-half quart of air. This accounts for approximately six quarts of air intake per minute. However, most people breathe too fast and too shallow. Improper breathing robs the body and organs of their full quota of air, which can inhibit function. Observe the breathing of those around you (or yourself) and notice how the shoulders and chests rise, but the bellies do not expand. This is improper breathing. Proper breathing is done slowly and deeply and the inhalation is felt all the way down into the lower abdomen. A good place to observe proper breathing is at a hospital's nursery. A healthy newborn breathes deep into his belly, it rises with each intake, and then slowly sinks upon exhaling. You do not see the shoulders or chest rise. Somewhere along the path to adulthood, we forgot how to breathe. Perhaps our response to all the reminders about walking tall with our shoulders high, chests out, and stomachs in were made at the cost of proper breathing.

Again, proper breathing involves filling the lungs completely and then exhaling completely. When the lungs have filled completely with air, the entire chest and abdominal area will expand. The actual amount of air taken into the lungs depends on an individual's cardiovascular endurance—the ability of the heart-lung system to transport blood and oxygen to the muscles during exercise. If an individual lacks cardiovascular endurance, this will limit the performance of techniques and other physiological actions during stressful situations.

Activities that require physical and mental exertion can place high levels of stress on the body. Life-threatening events, such as self-defense encounters, cause extreme levels of stress. When stress occurs, breathing can increase from six quarts of air per minute to one hundred and fifty quarts per minute. If you are not breathing properly, the demand on your system could jeopardize your ability to cope and effectively react.

During a defensive confrontation, stress-induced breathing will impair your fighting skills. In addition to the accelerated breathing, the stress of the encounter can bring about several physiological reactions, as mentioned, which include rapid heart beat, loss of reflexes, impaired vision or hearing, profuse sweating, diminished thought process, and loss of, or control of, speech and communication. The first step in calming these reactions is proper breathing.

Do not hold your breath during a self-defense encounter. Concentrate on taking deep breaths through your nose to allow the air to be filtered and warmed by the nasal cavity. Force the air down into the area of your *hara* or *tanden*. This is the lower abdominal area, just below the navel. The hara, according to Asian beliefs, is where all human life force or energy (*ki*) is located. Martial arts students are taught to focus their breathing in the hara, consolidating all physical and mental resources into and out of the place of energy. During a self-defense encounter you should be able to call upon these energies. This is accomplished by breathing deeply through the nose, forcing the air down into your hara. Exhale through the mouth forcefully, either with a *kiai* (shout), or with long exaggerated breaths. This practice is empowering, as it restores a sense of control, prepares you to take control of your physiological reactions, and finally take control of the confrontation.

Maintaining control of physiological actions enhances all skill levels. Training in deep breathing methods establishes the necessary rhythmic inhalation and exhalation process, making it easier to maintain proper breathing during a self-defense situation. The two prominent methods of deep breathing in karate training are *ibuki* and *nogare*. Both emphasize control of the abdominal area, and strengthen the diaphragm.

IBUKI BREATHING

FIGURE 3–1

FIGURE 3–2

FIGURE 3–3

FIGURE 3–4

Figure 3–1: Stand with your feet shoulder width apart; maintain an erect posture with your arms hanging relaxed at your sides.

Figure 3–2: Take a deep breath in through your nose, as you raise your arms up and across your chest to shoulder level, keeping your hands open.

Figure 3–3: Cross your arms, clench your fists, and tense your entire body. Set the breath in the lower abdominal area for a moment. Tense your abdominal muscles.

Figure 3–4: Form your hands into fists and slowly bring the arms down to your sides. Exhale through your mouth with force while maintaining tension in the abdominal muscles. When you feel as though all the air has been expelled, tense the abdomen even more and force out more air. Repeat this exercise two more times.

Ibuki should be used to restore breathing after strenuous exercise. It should also be used to restore breathing after sustaining a blow to the abdomen or diaphragm.

A note of caution: Athletes engaged in weight-lifting competition or training, where the objective is to lift the maximum weight possible, use a similar type breathing exercise. On occasion, some of the athletes have become light-headed and fainted. Some research shows that the fainting may be the result of the combination of deep-breathing, violent body movements during the lift, and increased blood flow. While there is no direct evidence that the deep-breathing exercise described above can cause strokes, some martial artists are leery, and therefore avoid this form of exercise. Always consult a physician before beginning any physical conditioning, martial art, or self-defense training.

NOGARE BREATHING

FIGURE 3–5   FIGURE 3–6

Figure 3–5: Stand with your feet shoulder width apart, and maintain an erect posture with your arms hanging relaxed at your sides.

Figure 3–6: Take a deep breath in through the nose as you raise your arms up to chest level, keeping the hands open.

FIGURE 3–7   FIGURE 3–8

Figure 3–7: Bring your hands alongside your chest as you force the air into your abdomen. Set the breath in your lower abdominal area for a moment.

Figure 3–8: With your tongue relaxed behind your upper teeth, exhale slowly. Maintaining the tongue in this position quiets the breathing. Repeat this exercise two more times.

Nogare is also referred to as combat breathing and should be used during jiyu-kumite (free fighting) and self-defense encounters because it is slow and quiet, with no telltale movement. This is important because you do not want to telegraph your breathing and give your assailant an opportunity to strike. Your body is vulnerable and weaker at the point of inhaling. When blocking a blow or delivering a technique, exhale with force and kiai—shout. Observe athletes during competition and you will see that they also use this form of breathing. Weight lifters are very audible as they exhale when pushing the weight. Even baseball and football players grunt, groan, or shout when they throw a ball or contact an opponent. They also realize that forceful exhaling makes the effort more effective and the body stronger.

Meditation

Periods of relaxation or meditation before and at the end of training sessions in the dojo are important for many reasons. First, they teach proper breathing techniques. During meditation, the student is guided to become aware of his or her breathing, with long, deep relaxed breaths taken in through the nose and out through the mouth. The student is further instructed to force the air into the hara and hold it there for a moment before exhaling. All mental and physical energies are focused on a single thought. This concentration of energies actually relaxes the mind, which is the second reason for meditation. A relaxed mind abandons all unnecessary thought. This no-thought or no-mind is known as *mushin*, and it is imperative during self-defense scenarios. In self-defense encounters you will not have time to think; you will only have time to react. If you cannot focus all your mental and physical energy without having to think, you will not be able to react effectively. Ask anyone who has survived a self-defense situation. They cannot tell you how or why it started, what transpired during the engagement, or how it ended. They cannot remember, not only because it happened too fast, but also because there was no time to think. Remember, if you have to think what to do or how to fight, you are losing. If you have not stopped your adversary within thirty seconds, you are probably going to lose. In losing, you can rest assured there will be injury and pain.

Pain

Students and instructors in self-defense training can expect to experience pain. This is crucial for real-life, practical, self-defense training. Pain is a warning signal that the body has been injured. The warning signal produced by pain is what facilitates our survival as we grow from childhood to adults. However, everyone does not experience pain in the same manner.

PAIN TOLERANCE

Some individuals are able to withstand more pain than others. They gain knowledge of how to react and handle their pain in different ways. Social conditioning from childhood can determine one's capacity to endure pain.

ACUTE PAIN

The interim pain that warns the body of a hazard comes on fast, and usually is the result of a specific strike or injury to the body.

CHRONIC PAIN

Pain that lasts over a long period of time is chronic pain. It is difficult to treat by a physician and can become unbearable.

Measuring pain is difficult and has restrictions, because some individuals can mentally block out pain. Extreme concentration may not allow pain sensations to reach your consciousness. When your concentration is interrupted, the pain is experienced. For example, soldiers during combat are often unaware of pain and severe injuries. They do not become aware of their pain or injuries until they are removed from the combat. Some do not even sense the pain of amputation.

PAIN RECEPTORS

The pain signals travel to the brain by electric currents in the nerves of the body. Pain receptors can be found in the skin and throughout the body. They tell the brain of imminent danger. These dangers include lacerations, broken bones, and other trauma, and the effects of heat and cold.

The electrical currents from pain receptors pass through the nerve fibers to the spinal cord and on to the brain. Nerve fibers are of two major categories: C-fibers, those that transmit pain, and A-beta fibers that transmit sensation. C-fibers are more abundant in the body than A-beta fibers and shape a network under the skin. A-beta fibers are larger and transmit sensations of pressure and touch.

GATE CONTROL

Children of very young ages, unaware of the physiological term, initiate *gate control* when they rub the part of the body that has been struck. This happens in the area of the spine where the C- and A-beta fibers come together. Here the painless A-beta fibers are apt to impede the pain traveling along the C-fibers. We continue to do this even as we mature. In most cases pain will disappear when the source is removed. The brain can only think of one thing at a time and can only experience one pain at a time.

Shock

The pain experienced during a self-defense confrontation can be the result of a severe blow, a broken bone, or a knife or gunshot wound. All of these injuries can produce bleeding. A blow to the torso area can rupture the kidney, spleen, or liver. A fractured bone can cause internal bleeding. The crucial element associated with bleeding is shock.

A person can lose one pint of blood during a brief timeframe without going into shock. A twenty percent loss of blood volume, approximately two pints, can cause the person to experience mild shock. A forty percent loss of blood volume, approximately four pints, can cause the person to experience severe shock. A stab or gunshot wound to the major arteries of the heart will bring on severe shock within five seconds. In many cases shock can be fatal, because it is so debilitating to the nervous system. Some of the symptoms of going into shock are restlessness (often the first indictor that the body is experiencing a significant problem); altered consciousness; pale, cool, moist skin; rapid breathing; and rapid pulse.

Voluntary and Involuntary Reactions

The nervous system has three major functions: orientation, coordination, and thought. We rely on unique senses to inform us of our location, or orientation, in a particular environment. The ability to orient to an ever-changing environment is what allows for our survival. Coordination allows us to collect information from nerve sensors, organize the information, and then select the proper course of action to be taken. Thought allows us to record, store, and relate information. This information is then used during future reactions to alterations in our environment.

A life-threatening situation, such as a self-defense confrontation, can cause a response that stimulates the central nervous system, the peripheral nervous system, and the autonomic nervous system. These stimuli to the various areas of the nervous system will result in voluntary and involuntary actions.

Voluntary actions stem from the central and peripheral nervous system and stimulate action in the muscles. Involuntary actions stem from the autonomic nervous system and are beyond conscious control. These various actions cause behavioral responses that produce a lack of balance amid the opposing nervous system responses. If this lack of balance occurs during a self-defense confrontation only one behavior can occur, fight or flight.

The fight-or-flight syndrome determines whether you will defend or flee. It is ludicrous to stand and fight in an altercation, regardless of the odds. No one can predict what will be going through a victim's mind during a life-threatening situation. The information being sorted out by the victim during the confrontation is what will determine the course of action. Training will be a huge factor in determining the action. Training must be intense, repetitive, and ongoing to produce a confident, capable response in which the individual will successfully be able to defend himself.

Pain can be your friend or foe, depending on how you accept it. If you yield to the pain, it then manifests as a psychological setback. The will to survive then waivers, or disappears completely. If you acknowledge the pain, it becomes a psychological boost. The will to survive becomes passionate. Many people have been seriously wounded in combat, and the way they dealt with the pain was the determining factor in whether they lived or died.

Intense physical conditioning and training strengthens our bodies and minds. Along with this strength, we develop a higher tolerance to pain. Can we learn to ignore the pain when we need to—during a life-threatening situation? Speaking from experience, I believe we can.

4

The Dojo Versus Real Life

How effectively a karate student responds in a fight, whether a tournament or a life-threatening street encounter, depends on his training. Remember the earlier account of the police officer? During a real-life shoot-out, he reverted to the way he trained and the result was fatal. The shoot-out placed the officer under an enormous amount of stress, the result of a life-threatening situation. Under this kind of stress, human beings will revert to measures they are comfortable with. This, again, is the dominant response. If your training is slow and sloppy, your fighting will be slow and sloppy. If your training is not realistic (involving contact), you will *not* survive a life-threatening self-defense encounter.

The majority of karate training today is geared toward sports and tournament competition. Although many karate schools advertise self-defense as a byproduct of their program, little, if any, training time is allotted for actual self-defense training. Emphasis is placed on tournament-style fighting. For the greater part, students are instructed to stop, or pull, their techniques just short of contact. They receive continuous reinforcement that contact is a foul, and illegal. This constant admonishment toward contact produces a non-contact response under actual self-defense conditions.

Another detrimental training technique is the *air-guitar syndrome*, or just going through the motions. Scores of martial arts students today only go through the motions when it comes to self-defense. They pair off and move in robot fashion up and down the dojo floor. One student plays the part of the attacker while the partner assumes the role of the defender. On the command from the instructor the assailant initiates an attack. The attack could come in the form of a single punch or kick, a combination of punches and kicks, a hold (headlock, bear hug, etc.), or a grab (lapel, hand, hair, etc.). The defender counters the attack with a series of hand and leg techniques, none of which make contact with the attacker. Yet, the attacking student obligingly falls to the floor or sails across the room (even when the attacker is twice the size and strength of the defender). This unrealistic training leaves the defender with the belief that their actions have actually rendered the attacker helpless. Boxers, amateur or professional, do not prepare for a match without engaging in several hours of contact sparring training. Without this contact training, they would not be prepared to defend and counter. Their bodies and minds would not be prepared for all the punches they will have to endure. Going-through-the-motions type training is a disservice to the students because it only instills a false sense of security.

My experience of forty years in the martial arts and twenty-five years as a defensive-tactics instructor to foreign and domestic military and law enforcement agencies, as well as engagements in life-threatening hand-to-hand combat situations has afforded me a first hand understanding of practical, real-life applications. As a defensive-tactics instructor, I trained many military and law enforcement personnel who came to me as experienced martial artists. If they had trained in karate schools that emphasized tournament-style training, they had difficulty adjusting to the realistic training that I was presenting. Many could not make adjustments and failed the programs. This was not because they were poor karate technicians. It was because they could not apply their techniques to real-life scenarios. Their problems were related to a multitude of training deficiencies. The most prevalent were issues of contact, focus, movement, and restrictions on rules of engagement.

- Contact: When struck, grabbed, or thrown to the ground, they did not react to the force put upon them. Many simply backed away, not countering or frozen with fear from the realization they had been struck hard and now had to seriously defend themselves.
- Focus: They lacked the ability to focus their energy into the various striking pads and apparatus with a penetrating force. When executing a counter, their techniques stopped short of their intended targets (called snapping or pulling back).
- Movement: Their direction of travel during a confrontation was strictly linear, moving forward or backward, with little or no side-to-side evasion tactics.
- Rules of Engagement: They were accustomed to wearing protective equipment, and when this element of security was removed they became tentative. They were also programmed to discontinue their attack after achieving what they believed was a scoring technique (a common tournament rule).

Contact is inevitable during a real-life self-defense encounter. The ability to stop, or at least stun, your opponent with a focused technique is a life-saving necessity. It is crucial to execute a technique or techniques while moving and changing directions. In addition, protective equipment does not exist in a street encounter. There is no padded safety mat on the ground, or someone to blow a whistle to stop the action and determine who scored. In a real-life self-defense situation the action is non-stop, brutal, sometimes deadly, and no one keeps score. Many readers may have had childhood scraps or brawls. You may recall that those "fights" ended up on the ground, often in a complete tangle. If you have ever viewed news footage or the real police television shows, you have seen that most of these encounters between an arresting officer and a suspect end up on the ground. Therefore, self-defense training must include ground fighting.

Self-defense training must also include the *what if* and *worst-case* scenarios. Put yourself into various scenarios and then envision defending yourself, for example, in the confines of your car, an elevator, or when comfortably nestled under the blankets on your bed. Attacks in these environments occur more often than most people think. The fright and psychological reactions a victim undergoes in these situations are inconceivable for the average person. Imagine settling in behind the wheel of your automobile, when suddenly an attacker grabs you from behind. Imagine being awakened from a sound sleep face-to-face with an assailant. As unfortunate as it is, this is reality. Your training should prepare you mentally and physically for such a reality.

5

Interrupting the Thought Process

An often-overlooked aspect of self-defense is the strategic element of interrupting the thought process of the assailant. Interrupting the thought process produces momentary lapses in judgment, physical-orientation and rhythm, and cardiovascular regularity. Any of these conditions brought on by a thought-interrupting technique may be all a victim needs to avoid a confrontation, or buy ample time to escape. However, before examining this topic there are specific human physiological traits of which one must be aware.

Muscle Control

No muscle works independently. A number of minute actions and muscle movements take place before and during the delivery of a technique. These specific actions and muscle movements are necessary for the technique to be delivered accurately and effectively.

For example, you are accosted when an individual grabs you by the arm, and launches into a verbal tirade. As the gravity of the incident increases, your attacker attempts to strike you with his opposite hand. The pressure exerted by the attacker on your grabbed arm will increase, or decrease, as he readies to strike you with his free hand. This is because other muscles needed to launch the strike have come into play. The noticeable change in pressure is minute, but it is noticeable. The additional muscle movement is also noticeable to the eye if you know what to look for. Like any applicable technique, this requires practice. Understanding these muscle mechanics will not only aide in the delivery of *your* techniques, it can enable you to block, avoid, or evade an *assailant's* techniques.

Breath Control

Proper breath control aides concentration, reduces stress, and assists in calming the body. The breathing pattern is also a telltale sign of vulnerability, or imperviousness to a counterattack. An attacker will inhale before launching his free-hand strike, because he needs to replenish the oxygen he has expended during exertion of the muscles of the arm, while applying the grab. One is most vulnerable during inhalation.

Almost everyone has experienced the following: You are walking in your own home; your mind is focused on another matter. Suddenly, a family member steps out and startles you. You jump back, taking a deep breath as you do. Now you begin to shake. You should have exhaled rather than inhaled. This would have had a more calming affect, and allowed you to react in a more positive manner. When an animal, wild or domesticated, is startled they react by growling, barking, or screeching, all the while exhaling. This is instinctive.

Pressure Points

Nerve endings, or pressure points, are located throughout the body and when hit, pinched, or squeezed they can cause extreme pain and motor dysfunction. The pain can actually cause mild to extensive shock to the nervous system. Attacking nerves, or other specific targets is much more effective than flailing about wildly or blindly. Throwing wild techniques, without power or aim, will not incapacitate an attacker, and it will also expend your energy quickly. This is why it is important to know which areas of the human anatomy are most vulnerable. These techniques are not secret, mysterious, or hard to learn.

Pressure-point manipulation and control is an extensive study in itself. The ability to deliver pain and debilitate an attacker using pressure-point tactics requires a thorough understanding of the nervous system. This includes the most vulnerable nerves, and the location of the most accessible nerves—those outside the skull and spinal column—the peripheral nervous system.

Inflicting pain and trauma by striking the nerves of an assailant can be crucial to survival. Some nerves, known as sympathetic nerves, when struck, trigger other nerve reactions. Striking the nose causes the eyes to tear, impairing vision. A finger in one eye causes both to close. These sympathetic reactions may delay an attacker's next move long enough for you to flee.

Here are some pressure points that may be useful in a self-defense situation. Again, the ability to accurately use these points takes many years of training.

FIGURE 5–1

FIGURE 5-2

FIGURE 5-3

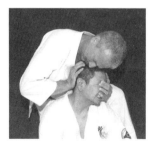
FIGURE 5–4

FIGURE 5-5

FIGURE 5–6   **FIGURE 5–7**

Figure 5–1: Pressure to nerve in the hollow behind the ear.

Figure 5–2: Pressure to nerve at the base of jaw.

Figure 5–3: Pressure to the nerve along the nasal cavity.

Figure 5–4: Pressure to the nerve along the nasal cavity and under the lip at the same time.

Figure 5–5: Pressure to the nerve along the throat.

Figure 5–6: Pressure to the nerve in the hollow of the throat.

Figure 5–7: Attack to the nerves on the top of the hand to break free of a hold. Form a fist and place the knuckles of your second joints against the assailant's hand. With your other hand grab your fist and push, twisting your knuckles into the hand of the assailant.

Techniques for Interrupting the Thought Process

If you can disrupt the thought process or the action of your attacker, you can destabilize or stop the technique from being completed. In dojo fighting, this strategic tool is often used to maintain control of the fight—making your opponent fight your fight. Thought-interrupting techniques are not difficult to learn or apply, and they work. This could include feinting with techniques or body movement, causing your attacker to shift his attention or his weight. It could be as subtle as a movement of the head or a change in eye direction. Alternatively, it could be intense, such as poking him in the eye with your finger. The body feels only one pain at a time and this requires a thought process. Every time the attacker receives a sudden new pain in a different place, a thought process has been interrupted. That is when you have the opportunity to break free, counter attack, or run. If you are able to interrupt your attacker's thought process, you will make him fight your fight. The following are choreographed examples that involve interrupting the thought process during self-defense encounters.

EXAMPLE 1

Your attacker, facing you, seizes you by the lapel. You strike, punch, and push against his arm trying to escape his grasp. You attempt to bend his arm in order to bring him closer so you can strike his face. You are no match for his size and strength and your actions prove fruitless. You need to disrupt his focus. At this time it is imperative that you perform one simple technique to interrupt his thought process. This could be a light slap to the face or body, asking him a question, or a light kick to his leg, which we will use for this example. The next technique and those following will be the primary counter attacks. Caution: Do not touch the arm that your attacker is using to hold you. Kick your opponent anywhere on his leg, the kick does not have to be full-force, then immediately drive your forearm or elbow down into the area of his elbow-joint with all your force. Now you are able to bend his arm. The thought-interruption (kick) took his mind off of his arm, just long enough for you to bend his arm.

> NOTE: It is important that you follow up immediately after the diversionary strike (in this case the light kick) that interrupts the thought –process. There can be *no* hesitation, or it will not work. (This technique will be shown with a series of photographs in Chapter 13: Escapes from Holds and Grabs.)

EXAMPLE 2

Your attacker grabs you in a side headlock, bending you over and down against his hip. Many individuals in this situation attempt to free themselves by trying to lift their attacker off his feet; this may work if the attacker is small or not very strong. Others try to push against his arm, or try to pry off his arms, all to no avail. The pain from a headlock is extreme and can eventually cut off the blood-flow to your brain and render you unconscious. Remember, you need to understand where his focus is and how to interrupt his thought process. Try the following: With the hand farthest from your attacker, strike the area surrounding his knee (this is the diversionary strike), immediately follow up by reaching up to his face with your other hand, dig your fingers deep into his eyes or into his nasal passages, and yank his head back as hard as possible, taking him to the ground.

> NOTE: It is important that you maintain contact with his face until you have taken him to the ground. The pain inflicted by your continuous assault to his eyes and nasal passage will distract him. By focusing on the pain, he will be less likely to think (thought interruption), or kick, or punch you. (This technique will be shown with a series of photographs in Chapter 13: Escapes from Holds and Grabs.)

Training

To better understand the act of interrupting the thought process, practice the following partner exercise.

FIGURE 5–8   FIGURE 5–9   FIGURE 5–10

Figure 5–8: Your opponent tenses his arm, resisting your attempt to force him to the ground. Grab your opponent's arm and as he resists, attempt an arm-bar takedown (see Chapter 11: Throws and Takedowns). You will notice that it is very difficult to execute.

Figure 5–9: Now try it with a diversionary technique. Kick either of your opponent's legs (the kick does not have to be full-force to interrupt his thought process).

Figure 5–10: Immediately follow the kick with the arm-bar takedown (Figure 5–10). At this point you should be able to accomplish the takedown. Reverse roles with your partner and continue the exercise.

Actions and techniques that interrupt the thought process confuse the assailant for the briefest moment. They must be followed immediately by a barrage of counterattacks. There can be no hesitation between the thought-interrupting maneuver and the counterattack. You cannot allow the assailant to regain his composure. You must be aggressive. Once you commit, do not stop!

6

Distance and
Body-and-Foot Movement

Maai (distance) and *sabaki* (body-and-foot movement) are two of the most important elements of self-defense training. Distance is the space between you and your attacker. Body-and-foot movement is the action. Both must be understood for you to fully appreciate how to avoid an attack while maintaining proper distance to execute your counter. Both must be practiced and performed simultaneously. There are two important rules to remember during any fighting situation. First, when your assailant delivers an assault, *do not be there*. Second, make your opponent fight your fight, *do not fight his fight*.

Do Not Be There

This refers to avoidance. At the precise moment your assailant attacks, move out of his line-of-attack. This requires that you remain calm and read the attack. Most people who are untrained in combative skills will telegraph their intent: they make a slight movement just prior to executing their technique that lets their opponent know what they are going to do. There are a variety of ways people telegraph. Their breathing rhythm might change. They might grunt, groan, sigh, or even speak. Or the telegraph could be as simple as a shift in weight, or the flexing or tensing of a body part. Watch for telltale muscle motion. The ability to read an opponent and detect telegraphing can only be achieved through proper and on-going training, just as the ability to deliver techniques without telegraphing can only be achieved through proper and on-going training. Once you are able to read your opponent's intent, moving out of his line-of-attack will become easier.

Do Not Fight His Fight

It is advisable to learn a variety of methods for moving off the line of attack, or taking evasive action. The method of sabaki that you use will be dictated by the attack. You may have to jump out of the way to avoid an attack, or clear an obstacle that is present. You may have to drop to the ground to avoid the assault. You may find that moving or angling your body by the slightest margin is all that is necessary. The method you employ, however, should not place you in a position that makes you more vulnerable. Your sabaki should also allow you to maintain your balance and your ability to counterattack. All forms of sabaki should be practiced in the dojo and should be applicable for the street.

In a street confrontation you will not have the luxury of the safe setting of the dojo. There will be no pads or mats to break your fall. You will not be able to call "time-out" or don protective equipment. There may be obstacles, such as walls, curbs, utility poles, mailboxes, table and chairs, automobiles, or people, which may limit or restrict your evasive movements. Train, plan for the worst conditions, and have contingencies.

FIGURE 6–1   FIGURE 6–2   FIGURE 6–3

During any type of fighting, you must constantly evaluate and change the distance between you and your attacker. You may have to use *all* distance conditions, long-range, short-range, and close-range, during the confrontation. If your assailant attacks with kicks or uses a weapon, such as a stick or bat, initially you are facing a long-range attack (Figure 6–1). This may work, but you may still be facing an onslaught of attacks. To neutralize the attacker, you may have to shorten the distance by using a mid-range movement (Figure 6–2). You can close the gap between you and your attacker, reducing the effectiveness of his weapon. If your assailant attacks with a shove, push, or punch you are facing a short-range attack. You may choose to defend at first by using a short-range movement, then by distancing yourself and moving just out of harm's way but allowing yourself to remain close enough to strike. A long-range distance will allow you to counter with kicks. If your assailant attacks with a grab or hold, or if you find yourself in a confined environment, this is a close-range situation (Figure 6–3). In these types of incidents your movements and distance are highly restricted and you may find that many attempts to use sabaki or maai are useless. This is why your training should always include contingencies.

Unarmed versus armed—what is the best distance to use in these situations? I am repeatedly asked this question wherever I instruct. My answer is always the same, "There is no best distance."

It would stand to reason that if you are unarmed and facing an armed assailant you would want to employ the long-range distance. Although this distance prevents you from receiving a wound inflicted by the weapon (unless the weapon is a firearm), it does not afford you the ability to control the weapon. In this case, if you have no other recourse but to defend yourself, you must use the short-range distance in order to control the weapon and neutralize the assailant. This requires that you close the gap between long-range and short-range as fast as possible. The mid-range distance is the danger-zone when a weapon (other than a gun) is in play, and you do not want to be there any longer than necessary. When facing an armed assailant you want to arm yourself, if possible, as soon as you can. At least, get some everyday item between you and the weapon as soon as possible.

In a situation where you are able to arm yourself with an everyday item (magazine, comb, brush, pen) to defend against an unarmed assailant the applicable distance is mid-range to short-range. Have the weapon at the ready. If the assailant taunts you or attempts to move at you, but does not fully commit, use the weapon to threaten him. This is done verbally. Do not wave or thrust the weapon in the direction of the assailant. Keep it close to your body. You do not want the assailant to take the weapon from you. Again, if there is no recourse and you must defend yourself, you need to be at the short-range distance to use the weapon.

Training

Alternating between the various methods of movement and distance during training will allow you to become aware of the pros and cons of each tactic. Training should include short-range and long-range jumps for proper distance, and actions where only one foot can move. It should also include actions where both feet remain in place and you only move your upper body. Movement and distance training should not be limited to standing upright. Dropping to the ground may be your only recourse for avoiding an attack. Once you are on the ground, there are techniques that will allow for safe movement and distance. Training should account for all such situations.

If you feel unstable or unbalanced with a new movement, or if it places you in a position where you cannot counter, modify the movement or distance. You may find that certain movements, such as going to the ground, restrict or reduce the effectiveness of certain techniques. Through training and practicing, learn what techniques are least affected by, or vulnerable to, changes in positioning and use them.

Shortening the Stick

Another form of distance training is known as shortening the stick. You may begin a long-range kick, punch, or strike, only to find the distance has closed between you and your attacker. You should be able to modify your technique in the middle of the execution without moving or changing distance. For example, a front kick with the foot becomes a knee kick. A punch or strike with the hand becomes an elbow strike.

Distance and foot and body movement are crucial elements of self-defense. Incorporating all forms of movement and distancing in your training will produce comprehensive, productive results for self-defense. Varying the way you move and the amount of distance you use builds balance and stability.

In a self-defense scenario, the way you move and the distance you choose can either confuse your assailant, or warn him of your experience and confidence levels. You must choose your tactics carefully, and employ them at the appropriate time.

7

Physical Fitness

Physical fitness is the key for sustaining a sense of confidence and well-being. If everyday, routine activities leave you fatigued and exhausted then your value of life is suffering. This exhaustion and fatigue will not permit you to participate in other activities designed for physical fitness and personal enjoyment. We have all heard the phrase, *sound body, sound mind*. When the body is in shape, the mind is in shape. When an individual can carry out routine activities without exhaustion and fatigue, mental stress is eliminated. Without the physical fatigue and mental stress, routine and personal enjoyment activities are limitless.

Physical fitness is essential in the training of martial arts and self-defense. If your physical fitness level is inadequate, your martial arts and self-defense techniques will be inadequate. No matter what your skill level, in the martial arts or self-defense, your tactics will be of little use if you do not possess adequate strength, power, flexibility, and stamina.

During life-threatening self-defense situations your mind and body, as well as those of the assailant, experience extreme changes. Two of these changes are an increased surge of adrenalin and an increased level of stress, both of which place high strain on the body. Adrenalin surges during self-defense produce both positive and negative results. On the positive side, power and energy is increased. However, this increase is short lived if your physical fitness level is poor. On the negative side, the assailant also experiences the adrenalin surge, which increases the power level of the assailant. Techniques against the assailant must be executed with more force than ever practiced in the dojo. If you have not stopped or incapacitated your attacker within thirty seconds, you are losing.

Physical fitness is also the key to a well-balanced life. It is obtained only through proper conditioning exercises. Cross-training in activities such as weight lifting, running, biking, or swimming should be a part of every martial artist's regimen.

The following physical conditioning exercises increase strength, power, cardiovascular endurance (stamina), and flexibility. The exercises should be performed every other day. Begin with three sets of ten repetitions each. As your condition improves increase the number of repetitions.

PUSH-UPS

Push-ups strengthen the pectoral (chest) muscles, as well as the shoulders and arms. They can be performed on the palms, knuckles, and fingertips.

FIGURE 7–1   **FIGURE 7–2**   **FIGURE 7–3**

Figure 7–1: This is the starting position of the fist-formed push-up on a makiwari board. Palms rest on the floor with the hands a little wider than the shoulders. Legs are extended, the back is straight, and the head is up.

Figure 7–2: Bend at the elbows and as you inhale, lower your chest to within two inches of the floor.

Figure 7–3: Push against the floor, and as you exhale, and raise your body. Repeat the exercise.

SIT-UPS

Sit-ups can strengthen the abdominal (stomach) muscles, as well as the lower back.

FIGURE 7-4   **FIGURE 7-5**

Figure 7–4: Lie on the floor with your legs bent at the knees. Place your hands behind your head and take a deep breath.

Figure 7–5: Exhale and raise your body until your shoulder blades are off the floor. Do not pull on your head during the exercise. Inhale and lower your back to the floor. Repeat the exercise.

Flexibility

Flexibility or stretching, enhances balance, speed, strength, power, and range-of-motion. Flexibility exercises should be performed after each workout. Hold the stretches for a minimum of thirty seconds. Avoid ballistic-type (bouncing) stretching.

HAMSTRING (HURDLER'S) STRETCH

FIGURE 7–6   FIGURE 7–7

Figure 7–6: Sit on the floor with the leg to be stretched extended out in front. Place the sole of the opposite foot against the inside of the thigh of the extended leg.

Figure 7–7: Take a deep breath and exhale. As you exhale, lower your chest toward the extended leg. In the beginning, you may not be able to get your chest all the way to the leg. Lower your chest only to the point where you feel the stretch in the back (hamstring) muscle of your leg. *Do not allow the knee of the extended leg to bend during the stretch.*

PECTORALS (CHEST)

FIGURE 7–8

STRETCH

Figure 7–8: Extend your arms to the rear and interlock your fingers. Gradually raise your arms until you feel the stretch in the pectoral (chest) muscles. This exercise stretches the muscles of the chest and the front shoulder muscles and will enhance all hand and arm techniques.

SHOULDER-GIRDLE STRETCH

FIGURE 7–9

Figure 7–9: Extend your arms to the front, interlock your fingers, and turn your palms outward. Push forward with your hands and at the same time push your shoulder blades to the rear. This exercise stretches the muscles surrounding the shoulder blades and enhances all hand and arm techniques.

Conditioning on an Apparatus

Various types of training equipment are available to the martial artist. Use of equipment is advantageous and the rewards are beneficial. Proper training utilizing the heavy-bag, makiwari board (Asian striking device), striking shields, and focus mitts helps develop hand-eye coordination, timing, movement, and distancing. This also strengthens the body and helps develop power and stamina.

The following photographs illustrate various training equipment items and their uses. Once you feel comfortable using the equipment, you can develop personal training regimens that suit your needs. The only limitation is your imagination.

HEAVY BAG

FIGURE 7–10

FIGURE 7–11

FIGURE 7–12

FIGURE 7–13

FIGURE 7–14

FIGURE 7–15

FIGURE 7–16

FIGURE 7–17

FIGURE 7–18

Figures 7–10 through 7–17: One partner steadies the bag while the other partner executes a combination of techniques: one-two punch, followed by two leg-kicks with the same leg, followed by a knee kick, then a front kick, and concluded with a forward elbow strike. In this form of training, the exercise is timed. The durations can vary from a few seconds to several minutes, depending on the student's endurance level. The student repeats the series of combinations as many times as possible in the allotted time. Training on the heavy bag increases power, strength, and cardiovascular endurance, while enhancing focus, timing, distancing, and body-and-foot movement. The benefits derived make the heavy bag an essential tool in a student's training regimen.

Figure 7–18: The students begin their combination routine as described above, only this time simultaneously. In this fashion, the bag moves and the students move and rotate in various directions around the bag. This method enhances focus, timing, distancing, and body-and-foot movement.

STRIKING SHIELDS

FIGURE 7–19

FIGURE 7–20

FIGURE 7–21

FIGURE 7–22

FIGURE 7–23

FIGURE 7–24

Figures 7–19 through 7–24: The student is working a combination routine, this time on the striking shield. The partner holding the shield can remain in one location or move about the floor in various directions. The latter is done whenever the holder feels like moving. This sporadic change in movement causes the working student to make quick adjustments in his distancing, timing, and body-and-foot movements. In another variation, the working student executes a preset number of repetitions of a single technique with the same hand and arm, or foot and leg. When this is complete he repeats the routine with the opposite arm or leg. The benefits derived from the striking shield are the same as the heavy bag.

Focus Mitts

Figure 7–25

Figure 7–26

Figure 7–27

Figure 7–28

Figures 7–25 through 7–28: The students are working a combination routine using focus mitts. The routine can be performed in the same manner as the heavy bag and striking shields. The use of the focus mitts brings the added benefit of allowing for simultaneous multiple targets. The benefits derived from focus mitt training are the same as with the heavy bag and striking shield.

MAKIWARI

FIGURE 7–29

FIGURE 7–30

FIGURE 7–31

FIGURE 7–32

FIGURE 7–33

FIGURE 7–34

FIGURE 7–35   **FIGURE 7–36**

Figures 7–29 through 7–36: The hand-held makiwari is a three-foot length of 2" x 6" board, wrapped with rope. It can be used in the same fashion as the heavy bag, striking shield, and focus mitts, and the benefits are the same. The exception is that the makiwari is solid, and therefore the focus (or penetration) is greatly enhanced. Because of its solid nature, acclimation to the makiwari must be gradual. Beginning students use light bouncing blows. As experience and conditioning levels increase, so will the impact level the student generates upon contact. The makiwari also toughens the skin of the various body parts employed during the training.

Peak physical condition requires maintaining a multi-faceted training schedule on a regular basis. Many assume that in order to achieve peak performance several hours each day must be dedicated to training. This is not true. Too much training can produce negative results. Here, once again, quality versus quantity is the issue. A good rule of thumb is to train every other day, and allow the body to rest, recuperate, and regenerate on the off days. If you feel you must train every day, then alternate the intensity level, and the particular exercise. An example would be weight resistance and cardiovascular training. Weight train on day one, do cardio training on day two, and continue to alternate in this fashion throughout the week.

Weight-resistance training should be done every other day. In order for muscles to grow, thus producing greater strength levels, they need at least twenty-four hours rest. This is true whether your purpose is to build bulk and strength or definition and muscular endurance. Bulk and strength require low reps and heavy weight. Definition and endurance require high reps and low weights. The benefits of weight training include increased energy levels, reduced body fat, and increased muscular flexibility, and strength.

Cardiovascular endurance (stamina) is achieved through running, swimming, biking, power-walking, and timed exercises (combination technique sequences on the heavy bag, striking shield, focus mitts), all of which are aerobic. To maintain optimum performance, cardio training requires that you maintain an intensity level of 60 to 75 percent of your maximum heart rate for a minimum of twenty minutes. The benefits of cardiovascular fitness include increased energy levels; decreased cholesterol, blood pressure, and stress; reduced body fat; and increased muscular flexibility and strength.

When you are in shape physically, you are in shape mentally. You feel good about yourself, and it shows in your posture and your outlook on life. Physical fitness is the key to sustaining a sense of confidence and well-being for a well-balanced life.

8

The Body's Arsenal

In the practice of traditional karate, which emphasizes self-preservation, the evolutionary process of training turns the practitioner's entire body into a weapon. The techniques (punches, strikes, kicks) should be basic and well-focused, but they should also be reactionary to the point of being instinctive. Complex and flashy techniques, especially high kicks, should be shunned. High kicks aimed to the head, or spinning-jumping kicks may look good in the dojo and in Hollywood movies, but they are impractical for self-defense. Kicking to the head weakens your balance and power. Limit your kicks to the attacker's head only after you have executed an initial technique that brings his head to your belt-level or lower.

There are many factors present during an encounter on the street that are absent in the safe confines of the dojo. One example would be restrictive clothing and footwear. Dress pants, jeans, and skirts reduce your flexibility and mobility, and the same is true for the layers of clothing (underwear, outerwear, sweater, jacket, or coat). The type of material in the soles of shoes may grip the ground prohibiting quick pivoting and maneuvering. Or the soles may be slick, like leather, and cause you to slip or lose traction. These are just a few of the factors that must be taken into account during a real-life violent encounter on the street.

Techniques for countering an attack must be kept simple in order to be effective for self-defense. Effective counter techniques can be done with any part of the body, once the body is trained properly. The following is a list of techniques, which depict the use of the entire body as an arsenal of weapons. These counter techniques are somewhat easier to learn than others, and therefore are more quickly honed into powerful and effective responses.

SEIKEN—FORE-FIST (FIST PARALLEL TO THE GROUND)

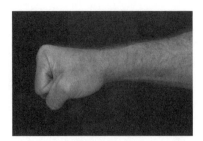

FIGURE 8-1 Side view   FIGURE 8-2 Front view

The points of contact in this technique are the knuckles of the index and middle fingers. Your fist must be in a straight alignment with the wrist and forearm upon contact to prevent injury.

Seiken chudan-tsuki (Fore-fist middle punch)

FIGURE 8–3: Front view   FIGURE 8–4: Side view

The Seiken chudan-tsuki, or fore-fist middle punch, is executed with the strong-side arm, and from a fighting position similar to that of a boxer. In Figure 8–3, the fore-fist punch is being delivered to the center of the opponent's body. The fore-fist punch can be delivered at an upward, middle, lower, and even a circular (hooking) direction. From a normal defense position (fists up near your face), palms inward, the striking arm extends out, the fist rotates fast (palm down) at the instant the first two knuckles make contact with the target.

The following photographs show the various real-life applications of the fore-fist punch.

FIGURE 8-5   FIGURE 8-6   FIGURE 8-7

Figure 8–5: Lead-side fore-fist punch to the jaw.

Figure 8–6: Strong-side fore-fist punch to the solar plexus.

Figure 8–7: Strong-side, circular (hook) fore-fist punch to the floating ribs.

TATEKEN—VERTICAL FIST

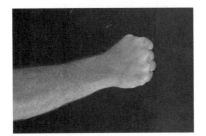

FIGURE 8–8: Side view   FIGURE 8–9: Front view

The points of contact in this technique are the knuckles of the index and middle fingers. Your fist must be in straight alignment with your wrist and forearm upon contact to prevent injury.

Tateken Jodan-uchi (vertical upper strike)

FIGURE 8–10: Front view   FIGURE 8–11: Side view

This punch is delivered straight to the target *without* rotating the fist upon contact.

The following photographs show the various real-life applications of the vertical fist strike.

FIGURE 8–12

FIGURE 8–13

Figure 8–12: Lead-side vertical strike to the jaw. Note the fist does not rotate on impact with the target.

Figure 8–13: Strong-side vertical strike to the solar plexus. Again, the fist *does not* rotate on impact.

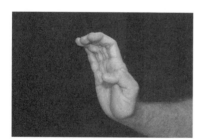

FIGURE 8–14: side view

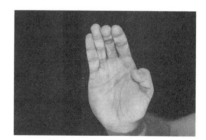

FIGURE 8–15: Front view

SHOTEI—PALM HEEL

The contact point in this technique is the heel of the palm. The thumb and fingers are relaxed and the hand is snapped back just at the point of contact, forcing the power into the palm-heel for full impact into the target.

Shotei ago-uchi (palm heel chin strike)

FIGURE 8–16   FIGURE 8–17

The palm heel strike to the jaw (Figure 8–16) is executed with the lead-side arm and hand. The striking hand travels out from its position near your face toward the target. Snap the striking hand fingers back at the moment of contact. This allows the heel of the hand to snap forward, allowing for penetration of force into to the jaw. *Do not* push your palm heel against a target. The delivery of the palm heel strike to the mid-section (Figure 8–17) is the same as to the jaw. *Do not* push your palm heel against the target.

The following photographs show the various real-life applications of the palm heel strike.

FIGURE 8–18   FIGURE 8–19   FIGURE 8–20

Figure 8–18: Palm heel strike to the assailant's jaw, executed with the lead-side arm/hand.

Figure 8–19: Palm heel strike to the assailant's groin, executed with the strong-side arm/hand.

Figure 8–20: Palm heel strike to the assailant's solar plexus, executed with the strong-side arm/hand.

TETSUI—HAMMER FIST

The contact point in this technique is the bottom edge (fleshy part) of the hand, opposite the thumb. The hammer fist strike can be executed to the front or rear with either the strong-side or lead-side arm/hand, and to the right and left in a lateral direction.

Tetsui Oroshi-uchi (descending hammer fist strike) and Tetsui Sayu-uchi (lateral hammer fist strike)

FIGURE 8–21: Front view   FIGURE 8–22: Rear view

The descending hammer fist strike (Figure 8–21) is executed with the strong-side arm/hand to the top of the assailant's head. The hammer fist strike should drive through the target. *Do not* snap the fist back upon contact.

In the case of the lateral (left, right) hammer fist strike (Figure 8–22), the strike is being delivered with the left hand, although the strike can be delivered in this manner with either side hand. The hammer fist strike should drive through the target. *Do not* snap the fist back upon contact.

The following photographs show the various real-life applications of the hammer fist strike.

FIGURE 8–23   FIGURE 8–24   FIGURE 8–25

Figure 8–23: The victim, grabbed by the assailant, executes a hammer fist strike in a descending direction against the forearm of the assailant's arm.

Figure 8–24: The victim executes a hammer fist strike to the assailant's head as he attempts to grab her.

Figure 8–25: Grabbed from the rear, the victim executes a hammer fist in a backward direction into the assailant's groin.

NUKITE—SPEAR HAND

The contact points in this technique are the fingertips with the tips of the fingers adjusted to be in full alignment with each other. Press your fingers firmly together, and press your thumb firmly against the index finger to add support. A variation of this technique is a two-finger (index and middle) strike aimed at the eyes.

Nukite Chudan-uchi (spear hand middle-level strike)

FIGURE 8–26: Front view   FIGURE 8–27: Side view

The fingers pressed firmly together and reinforced by the thumb give this weapon its strength. With the palm facing in, the fingertips are thrust into the mid-section.

Nukite Jodan-uchi (spear hand strike to throat)

FIGURE 8–28: Side view

With the palm facing down, the fingertips are thrust into the throat.

The following photographs show the various real-life applications of the spear hand strike.

FIGURE 8–29

FIGURE 8–30

Figure 8–29: Victim executes a strong-side spear hand strike to the assailant's solar plexus.

Figure 8–30: Victim executes a lead-side spear hand strike to the assailant's throat.

NIHON NUKITE—TWO-FINGER SPEAR HAND

The two separate contact points in this technique are the fingertips of the index and middle fingers. This is the variation of the spear hand strike mentioned earlier.

Nihon Nukite Jodan-uchi (two finger strike to the eyes)

FIGURE 8–31: Side view

The victim executes a strong-side two-finger (index and middle) spear hand strike to the assailant's eyes. The technique is executed in a follow-through fashion. This defense can temporarily blind the assailant, while activating various sympathetic nerves allowing the victim to flee.

HIJI—ELBOW

The contact point in this technique, depending on the execution and direction of the strike, can be either just below or just above the elbow. The contact point is *not* the tip of the elbow or the bone itself. The elbow strike can be delivered in a forward horizontal, rising vertical, rearward, or descending motion.

Hiji Jodan-uchi (strong-side elbow upper-level strike)

FIGURE 8–32: Side view

From the normal defensive posture (hands up near face), the elbow travels forward in a circular motion, and follows through the target.

Hiji Chudan-uchi (lead-side elbow middle-level strike)

FIGURE 8–33: Side view

This strike is delivered in the same manner as the upper-level strike.

Hiji Ushiro-uchi (rear elbow strike to mid-section)

FIGURE 8–34: Side view

Drive either side elbow to the rear. The opposite hand pushes against the striking-side fist to add extra momentum and power. Follow through on contact with the target.

The following photographs show the various real-life applications of the elbow strike.

FIGURE 8–35   FIGURE 8–36   FIGURE 8–37

Figure 8–35: Strong-side forward elbow strike to the assailant's head.

Figure 8–36: Lead-side forward elbow strike to the assailant's ribcage.

Figure 8–37: Rear elbow strike to the assailant's mid-section. Alternate between the left-side and right-side strikes until you are free.

NOTE: The elbow strike is an excellent weapon for attacking an assailant's hands and arms if he is attempting to grab you. With your hands up near your face, swing your elbow forward as you rotate your hips, and strike the assailant's outstretched hand or arm with an elbow strike. Continue the rotating action of the hips and deliver a barrage of elbow strikes, alternating between your left and right side.

ATAMA—HEAD

The contact points in this technique are the upper portion of the forehead (the crown) and the back and side of the head.

Atama Shomen-uchi (forward head strike)

FIGURE 8–38: Side view

Thrust forward, driving your head through the target. The forward head strike can be delivered against any part of the assailant's body.

Atama Ushiro-uchi (backward head strike to face)

FIGURE 8–39: Side view

The following photographs show the various real-life applications of the head strike.

FIGURE 8–40   FIGURE 8–41

Figure 8–40: The victim delivers a forward head strike to the solar plexus of the assailant as he attempts to grab her.

Figure 8–41: Grabbed from the rear, the victim delivers a backward direction head strike against the assailant's face. In this situation, a good follow-up technique would be a series of rear elbow strikes.

Chosoku—Ball of the Foot

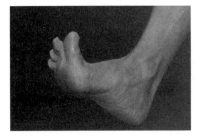

FIGURE 8–42: Side view

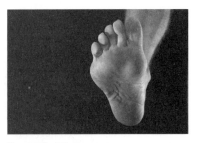

FIGURE 8–43: Front view

The contact point in this technique is the ball of the foot, formed when the toes are pulled back. Pulling back the toes tenses the foot, creates a hard-surface weapon, and reduces the risk of injuring your toes. This applies even when wearing shoes, although to a lesser extent.

Mae-geri (front kick)

FIGURE 8–44: Side view

The front kick can be executed with either leg. Raise the knee of your kicking leg and snap your foot forward. As the ball of the foot makes contact with the target, drive through, but *do not* push the foot. The front kick can be executed against any portion of an assailant's body. It is not recommended, however, that any kicks be delivered higher than the assailant's mid-section.

The following photographs show the various real-life applications of the front kick.

FIGURE 8–45   FIGURE 8–46

Figure 8–45: Front kick to the assailant's groin.
Figure 8–46: Front kick to the assailant's abdomen.

SOKUTO—BLADE OF THE FOOT

The outside edge (blade) of the foot is the contact point in this technique. Pull your toes back and turn your heel slightly outward.

Sokuto kensetsu-geri (knife kick to knee)

FIGURE 8–47: Front view

Raise the knee of the kicking leg as high as possible and then thrust the foot downward with force, striking with the blade of the foot.

The following photographs show the various real-life applications of the knife kick.

FIGURE 8–48   **FIGURE 8–49**

Figure 8–48: The victim delivers a knife kick to the outside of the assailant's knee.
Figure 8–49: The victim delivers a knife kick to the front of the assailant's knee.

HAISOKU—INSTEP

The instep (top of foot) is the contact point in this technique. Tense and point your toes.

KIN-GERI (GROIN KICK)

FIGURE 8–50: Side view

Raise the knee of the kicking leg and then snap the foot forward, striking the target with the instep.

Here is an example of the groin kick in a real-life situation.

FIGURE 8–5 I

Figure 8–51: Real-life application of the groin kick.

HIZA—KNEE

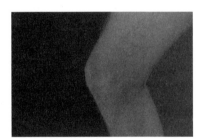

FIGURE 8–52: Side view

FIGURE 8–53: Front view

The contact point in this technique is the lower portion of the quadriceps (front thigh muscle), just above the knee. The contact point is *not* the patella (kneecap). It is important when executing the various knee kicks that you point your toes down. This assures full extension of the ligaments and tendons surrounding your knee, allowing for maximum range of motion during the kicks.

Hiza-geri (knee kick)

FIGURE 8–54: Side view

The knee kick can be executed with either leg in a forward or circular direction, against a variety of targets. As your knee rises drive it into the target with force.

The following photographs show the various real-life applications of the knee kick.

FIGURE 8–55   **FIGURE 8–56**   **FIGURE 8–57**

Figure 8–55: Forward knee kick to the groin/abdomen area of the assailant. Note that she pulls down on the assailant's shoulders in order to increase the momentum and power in the kick.

Figure 8–56: Forward knee kick to the assailant's face. Note that she pulls down on the assailant's shoulders bring his face within range.

Figure 8–57: Roundhouse (circular) knee kick to thigh of assailant.

SUNE—SHIN

The contact point in this technique is the shinbone. It is important when executing kicks that utilize the shin that the toes point downward. The shin is also an adequate defense against kicks aimed at the legs.

Gedan mawashi-geri (low roundhouse kick)

FIGURE 8–58: Side view

The knee of the kicking leg is raised high and pointing to the outside of the body. The kicking leg then whips in a circular motion to the target, driving through the intended target. The target for this kick is any part of the body that is hip-height or lower. The prime target is the knee.

Here's a look at a real-life application of the low roundhouse kick.

FIGURE 8–59

Figure 8–59: Real-life application of the low roundhouse kick, executed against the assailant's knee.

9

Everyday Weapons

The term "everyday weapon" applies to any weapon other than the natural weapons of the body, which are described in Chapter 8. *Any* item (newspaper, book, magazine, food seasonings, comb, hairbrush, aerosol sprays, purse, toothbrush, pencil, clothing, and more) can be used as weapon.

Aerosol Sprays

All aerosol sprays (hairspray, degreaser, paint, oil, and more) are useful tools for self-defense if they are immediately at hand. There are also personal-protection sprays (pepper, teargas, CS, etc.) available. Before purchasing a personal-protection spray, it is important to know the product's limitations. To be effective, sprays must be readily accessible. They are of *no use* if they are buried at the bottom of a purse, or wedged in a tight pocket. You will not have time to rummage through your purse or pocket during a violent confrontation,.

Aerosol sprays come in a variety of chemical ingredients. Some of these, such as cooking sprays, have no adverse effects on an assailant other than annoyance. Even the less effective compounds, however, including any spray that can harm or incapacitate, should be aimed at the face, in particular the eyes, nose, and mouth. Be aware that close proximity to the spray can also affect the individual discharging the spray.

Clothing

The clothing you wear can be effective for both defensive and offensive purposes. In the event you are attacked with a knife or other sharp instrument, you can remove your jacket or coat and wrap it around your arm to prevent being cut. You can also use a jacket, coat, or belt to lash out at the attacker as a means of distraction. They can also be used to block and parry attacks, and as a means to entangle an assailant. On another note, if the clothing you wear is tight fitting it can restrict your actions and movements. This is also true of high-heel shoes. Be aware of your attire and its limitations.

Briefcase, Gym Bag, and Purse

You can also use a briefcase, gym bag, or purse as a defense against a knife or other sharp instrument. Get the item between you and the attacker, or the weapon, as a means of defense or a distraction measure. Either item can also be swung or pushed at the attacker as an offensive measure.

Newspaper, Magazine, and Book

A newspaper, magazine, or book can become a good weapon if you are attacked. You can roll the newspaper or magazine for strength and stability.

The following photographs show the defensive application of various everyday items in real-life confrontations. Keep in mind that any of the weapons shown in the photographs can be replaced with whatever is at hand if you are attacked.

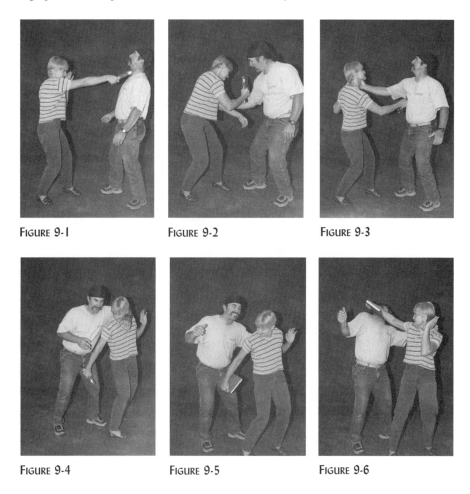

FIGURE 9-1   FIGURE 9-2   FIGURE 9-3

FIGURE 9-4   FIGURE 9-5   FIGURE 9-6

Figure 9–1: Rolled-up magazine or newspaper thrust against the throat.

Figure 9–2: Rolled-up magazine or newspaper thrust against the nerve on the forearm.

Figure 9–3: Rolled-up magazine or newspaper thrust into the assailant's armpit.

Figure 9–4: Rolled-up magazine or newspaper thrust backward into the assailant's groin.

Figure 9–5: Hardcover book thrust backward into the assailant's groin.

Figure 9–6: Hardcover book thrust backwards into the assailant's neck or face.

Comb, Hairbrush, Toothbrush, or Pen

These four everyday items are versatile defensive weapons. They are usually made of wood or hard plastic, and when properly used they can deliver a tremendous amount of focused energy on impact. They can be used in a thrusting or slashing type movement.

FIGURE 9–7   FIGURE 9–8

Figure 9–7: Hairbrush raked across the assailant's eyes and face.

Figure 9–8: Hairbrush handle thrust against the assailant's nose or eyes.

10

Falling

Falling is an integral part of all self-defense training. It is often overlooked, however, or emphasis is not placed upon it in many martial arts schools. Think back to your youth, when you or a friend became involved in a physical confrontation. If the confrontation escalated to a fighting situation, it was most assured that someone would fall. Similarly, finding yourself shoved or thrown to the ground during a self-defense situation is highly probable. Because of this, it is most important that you learn how to fall in order to prevent being injured.

Falling is another aspect of self-defense that differs greatly from training in the dojo. In the dojo one is dressed in a dogi, or other loose fitting attire that allows for easy movement when practicing falls. In the real world, movements are restricted by tight jeans, skirts, pantyhose, coats, and fashionable but impractical shoes. In the dojo, the floor is covered with rubberized safety mats to reduce injuries. There are no safety mats on the street. There is concrete and asphalt, gravel and sand, glass and debris, and painful outcroppings known as curbs. Your confidence can be short-lived when your body slams against the hard, immovable ground.

Injuries ranging from minor to serious can occur when falling on objects, such as glass, gravel, curbs, and the hard pavement. Injuries sustained from falling on any of these objects could cause incapacitation, leaving you immobile, and at the mercy of your assailant. In addition, if you are less mobile, escape options are limited, and your assailant can use the ground as a weapon, by pounding your head or body into submission. Whenever possible, avoid being taken to the ground.

Break Falls

In a break fall, you break or impede your fall by landing in a specific position, either slapping or attacking the ground with the muscles of your forearms and hands. Upon contact with the ground, your muscles absorb and displace the shock associated with the impact. It is important that the muscles, not the bones, make the initial contact. It is also important that once you begin a fall you *go* with it, rather than attempting to fight it.

FRONT BREAK FALL

FIGURE 10–1

FIGURE 10–2

Figure 10–1: This is the beginning position in the practice of a front break fall. Note that the hands are up, palms facing the floor.

Figure 10–2: This is the final position of a front break fall. When performing a front break fall *do not* drop to your knees. Prone out, and allow most of your body surface to contact the ground at the same time. Slap your palms and forearms on the ground at the same time to absorb the impact. Exhale as you hit the ground.

REAR BREAK FALL

FIGURE 10–3

FIGURE 10–4

Figure 10–3: The standing position is the beginning move in the practice of a rear break fall. Note that the arms are relaxed and the palms face the floor. Lower your center of gravity by bending your knees.

Figure 10–4: This is the final position of a rear break fall. Allow as much body surface to contact the ground as possible, and avoid landing on your coccyx (lowest portion of the spine). Slap your palms and forearms on the ground at the same time to absorb the impact. Exhale as you hit the ground.

SIDE BREAK FALL

FIGURE 10–6

FIGURE 10–5

Figure 10–5: The standing position is the beginning move in the practice of a side break fall.

Figure 10–6: This is the final position of the side break fall. Allow as much body surface to contact the ground as possible and avoid landing on the hip and knee. Slap your palm and forearm on the ground at the same time to absorb the impact. Exhale on contact with the ground.

ROLLOUT FALL

In the rollout fall, your movement continues in a specified direction upon contact with the ground. Use the momentum from a shove or throw to carry you to a safe conclusion of the fall (and hopefully a safe distance from your assailant). Unlike a break fall, where you come to a halt upon contact with the ground, a rollout does just as its name implies— roll out or away in the direction you are being carried by your momentum. During the application of rollouts, try to imagine yourself as a ball, round and smooth. Tuck in your arms, legs, and head, and become a ball, easy to maneuver, and roll away. Again, it is important that once you begin a fall you *go* with it, rather than attempt to fight it.

TWO-HAND FORWARD ROLLOUT

FIGURE 10–7

FIGURE 10–8

FIGURE 10–9

Figure 10–7: Begin the practice of a forward roll from a crouched position.

Figure 10–8: Place both palms on the floor and tuck your head. Push off with your feet and do a somersault. Roll onto your back. *Do not* make contact with the ground with your neck and head. Try to imagine you are a round ball.

Figure 10–9: This is the final position of forward roll. As you come out of the roll slap your palms and forearms on the ground at the same time to absorb the impact. Exhale on contact with the ground.

Proper falling allows you to contact a hard surface with minimal discomfort and this minimizes injuries. Falling is another important technique that requires repetitive training for one to become proficient.

11

Throws and Takedowns

Throws and takedowns are two of the most important tactical applications of self-defense. The objective of any self-defense encounter is the ability to stun or incapacitate your attacker. The sudden impact of your attacker being hurled against a stationary object may afford you the opportunity to flee or terminate any further aggression against you.

Many individuals who are untrained in self-defense, and even some novices who are trained, believe that individuals of smaller stature cannot successfully throw or take-down a larger opponent. These same individuals are also under the assumption that throws and takedowns are always aimed toward the ground. Neither of these assumptions are true.

Smaller individuals, with proper training, can easily throw or takedown a much larger opponent. If you have ever witnessed a professional football game, you have often seen smaller players upending or tackling larger players. They are able to accomplish this by getting under, and lower than the larger player. The same is true for throws and takedowns. The larger the attacker, the lower the defender must set his or her center of balance. Leverage, the principle element in all throws and takedowns, permit individuals of smaller stature to upend larger opponents. Once this concept is understood, practiced, and achieved, size is irrelevant.

When executing throws or takedowns in self-defense scenarios, several stationary objects can be used to your advantage. For example, you can direct your attacker against a wall, telephone pole, mailbox, fence, fire hydrant, or vehicle. All of these and any other stationary object that is present are substantial allies. The ground does not always have to be the termination point of a throw or takedown.

There are many types of throws and takedowns. The techniques shown here are basic, and with adequate practice they can be accomplished with relative ease.

Balance

Maintaining balance is necessary for the proper execution of a throw or takedown. Without good balance, the throw or takedown can become weak, minimizing its usefulness. Without good balance, you are also susceptible to injury, or to ending up on the ground with your assailant on top of you.

It is impossible to perform an effective throw or takedown from an off-balance position. In order to maintain your balance, employ a strong foundation by spreading your feet shoulder-width or slightly wider. Keep in mind that if your foundation is too wide it will have the same effect as not having your foundation wide enough—you will be off-balance.

Again, the most effective way to maintain your balance is to spread your legs shoulder width or slightly wider, flex your knees, bend at the hips—not the waist and do not lean your upper body more than thirty-five degrees in any direction. There are several exercises you can practice to enhance your balance.

1. Stand on one foot, sway back and forth, lean your upper body in various directions, and then flex the knee and perform squats. *Do not* allow the upper leg to bend farther than ninety degrees. Remember to do both sides.
2. Hop or make small jumps in various directions. Alternate between landing on one foot and the other, and on both feet. Increase the tempo as your balance improves.
3. Perform the same hopping exercise, but place objects of varying heights around you. Hop and jump over them.
4. With a partner, proceed through the various movements of a throw or takedown, but do not take it to completion. Halt at various stages in the technique, with your partner's full body weight on you. Shift your own weight in various directions. Lean and bend to determine the point-of-no-return—the moment just before you fall to the ground. Try spreading your legs to varying widths.

These exercises enhance strength, flexibility, and coordination. They bring an understanding of what is too much or not enough in the angle of the lean and the width of the stance when executing a throw or takedown.

Your Center of Gravity

You will also need to employ a low-center of gravity, the area just below your navel (tanden). To lower your center, bend your knees. Again, just as with the balance technique, too much of a good thing can be detrimental. If you bend your knees too much you will lower your center, but it will also begin to shift forward or backward, depending on the throw or takedown you are employing. Once again, you will be off-balance. When you bend your knees, keep your spine as straight as possible. This is accomplished by keeping your gaze upwards. One way to do this is by looking up at your opponent's face for as long as possible during the execution of the technique

In addition, as mentioned earlier in the section on balance, *do not* allow your upper body to lean more than thirty-five degrees in any direction, and *do not* allow the upper legs to bend more than ninety degrees.

The exercises listed in the Balance section are also beneficial for understanding and developing a good center of gravity.

Follow-Through

Another important aspect of keeping your balance is the follow-through. Maintain forward momentum with proper body rotation, and foot placement, throughout the completion of any throw or takedown. Once you have achieved the proper foundation and center-of-gravity, look to where you want your opponent to go, and then throw, or take him there. *Where the head goes, the body follows.*

Failure to follow through will lessen the effects of the throw or takedown. You may also injure yourself, or again, end up on the ground with the assailant on top of you.

Falling

Finally, if you find yourself falling along with your opponent, go with the fall. *Do not* attempt to fight the fall.

If possible, attempt to land on your assailant, and not the other way around. If you find yourself falling toward your assailant, make every attempt to hit him with your elbows and knees. Whether you land on top, underneath, or away from him, you have three options: keep fighting, subdue your attacker, or escape. The action you select must be immediate.

Techniques

There are numerous throws, takedowns, and submission techniques. The following are the more basic. They are easy to learn and practical for self-defense.

Hip Throw

FIGURE 11–1   FIGURE 11–2

FIGURE 11–3

Figure 11–1: Grasp your assailant's arm, spread your legs, bend your knees, and thrust your buttocks into his abdomen as you pull down on his arm.

Figure 11–2: Continue to pull the assailant's arm diagonally and downward across your body, and force your hip into his abdomen as you rotate your hip forward.

Figure 11–3: Slam the assailant to the ground while maintaining control of his arm.

SHOULDER THROW

FIGURE 11–4   FIGURE 11–5   FIGURE 11–6

Figure 11–5: Continue to pull the assailant's arm forward and down toward the ground, and force your hip into his abdomen.

Figure 11–4: Grasp your assailant's arm, spread your legs, bend your knees, and thrust your buttocks into his abdomen as you pull down on his arm.

Figure 11–6: Continue to pull his arm, sliding him across your back, and over your shoulder. Slam the assailant to the ground while maintaining control of his arm.

OUTSIDE REAPING THROW

FIGURE 11–7   FIGURE 11–8   FIGURE 11–9

Figure 11–7: Grasp the assailant's wrist and the shoulder of the same arm.

Figure 11–8: Kick the leg closest to your assailant forward and high into the air.

Figure 11–9: Bring your leg down hard against the back of the assailant's leg at the area of the knee or lower. At the same time, push forward into his shoulder as you pull down on his arm. Slam the assailant to the ground while maintaining control of his arm.

BACK-TO-BACK THROW

FIGURE 11–10   FIGURE 11–11

FIGURE 11–12   FIGURE 11–13

Figure 11–10: Grasp the assailant's wrist and the shoulder of the same arm.

Figure 11–11: With the leg closest to the assailant, step forward and behind him. Thrust your buttocks into his lower back. At the same time, slide your inside arm across the front of his neck.

Figure 11–12: Drive your forearm into the assailant's neck, pushing him back. At the same time continue to push your buttocks into his back as you pull down on his arm.

Figure 11–13: Continue to push and pull, bringing the assailant over your back. Slam the assailant to the ground while maintaining control of his arm.

ARM-BAR TAKEDOWN

FIGURE 11–14   FIGURE 11–15   FIGURE 11–16

Figure 11–14: Grasp your assailant's wrist. At the same time, with your opposite hand, place it against the back of his arm at the elbow. As you pull up on the wrist, push down on the elbow.

Figure 11–15: Drive your body into his armpit, pushing downward.

Figure 11–16: Slam the assailant to the ground while maintaining control of his arm.

HEAD-TWIST TAKEDOWN

FIGURE 11–17   FIGURE 11–18

Figure 11–17: Cup your hand over the assailant's chin. At the same time, grasp the back of his head with your other hand.

Figure 11–18: Pulling and pushing your hands in opposite directions will twist the assailant's head back and down. Slam the assailant to the ground while maintaining control of his arm.

Most physical confrontations place the assailant and victim within the short-range distance. Throws and takedowns are excellent self-defense techniques for this range. If applied properly they can stun or incapacitate the assailant—allowing you time to escape.

12

Ground Techniques and Fighting

It is highly probable that an attacker who is not immediately stopped or neutralized with a well-placed strike will continue fighting the victim to the ground. If this occurs, one must be prepared and capable of maintaining an effective defense.

Ground-fighting training in the dojo should place the student in all possible positions: prone, supine, and on his or her side. Most karate techniques practiced in an upright standing position can also be executed from the ground with only slight modifications. Ground fighting will show the effectiveness of the techniques even while on the ground, as well as the limitations.

The Pros and Cons of Ground Fighting

In a standing position, the legs create the strong foundation, or balanced stance. When students practice techniques from a standing position, they learn that a strong, well-balanced stance is essential for power in the execution of techniques, range-of-motion, and maneuvering. If techniques are not practiced from the ground, students will not learn to compensate for the lack of foundation. Once on the ground, the student realizes that without the solid ground against his feet he has no foundation, and he or she can learn how to adjust his techniques to maintain effectiveness. Ground-fighting training instills in the student the need to maintain a barrage of techniques against the assailant in order to regain a standing position as soon as he or she is able. Training on the ground also shows the student that it is not so easy to dislodge an attacker when all the attacker's weight is forcing down upon them.

An interesting scenario that can, and should, be practiced in the dojo follows. Ask a student to lie on the dojo floor and cover him or her with a blanket, as if they were at home sleeping in bed. Now, have another student play the attacker. The restrictive nature of the blanket greatly hinders the victim's ability to fight. In real life, the problem would be compounded by the softness of the mattress and the darkness. These added restrictions strictly limit the defensive measures. Practice this scenario and discover what techniques work and what modifications are required.

Although fighting on the hard ground can cause havoc to your body, restrict movement, and reduce the effectiveness of certain techniques, there are advantages associated with ground fighting.

Leverage, the key element in throws and takedowns, is also a key element in ground fighting. You can push against the ground with your hands, forearms, elbows, feet, legs, pelvis, and even your head and buttocks, in order to gain leverage over an opponent. When you press a specific body part against the ground, it creates a pivot point. This fulcrum provides momentum, and in turn leverage, which is then used against an opponent.

Going to the ground can also disorient your assailant by interrupting his thought process. This brief lapse in his attention may be all you need to launch an effective counter or escape. In addition, taking the assailant to the ground with you places him in a more vulnerable position.

The ground may also be your only course of escape. If your movement is obstructed by natural or fabricated structures, or by vehicles, your only option may be to go to the ground in order to roll away from an attack.

The final and most important advantage of ground-fighting training is the fact that most real-world self-defense scenarios culminate on the ground. If you are not prepared and trained for this inevitable episode you may panic, and the outcome could be fatal.

Cover and Avoidance Techniques

Ground-fighting training should also include cover and avoidance techniques. Covering and rolling movements can be used to avoid further assault, indoors or out, to roll under a car or a bed. In this segment of training, the student takes a position on his back on the dojo floor and brings his arms over his chest while covering his face with his palms. The palms do not rest on the face, but remain one to two inches above the face. Maintaining this position, the student rolls, back to front, continuing in this manner until he has negotiated the dojo floor The hard ground, or floor, wreaks havoc on the body, and this is another reason why all karate students need to maintain good physical condition.

Many martial arts and self-defense instructors are of the school of thought that ground-fighting techniques are not necessary. They justify this by telling anyone (especially unsuspecting students) that their art or system is so powerful and effective that no opponent will ever succeed in taking one of them to the ground. What nonsense! Avoidance maneuvers on the ground are just as important as standing techniques. Avoiding and distancing the attack are crucial elements of self-defense. Here are some important techniques to use if you find yourself on the ground.

COVER AND AVOIDANCE ROLLAWAY

FIGURE 12–1   FIGURE 12–2   FIGURE 12–3

Figure 12–1: Beginning position (prone). Bring your hands up to protect your head and use your forearms to provide momentum.

Figure 12–2: First revolution to back. Maintain the roll by pushing against the ground with your forearms and toes, or with the balls of your feet.

Figure 12–3: Second revolution returning to prone. Continue rolling until you are out of harm's way, or at a safe distance to rise and escape.

Ground Defenses

SIDE DEFENSE POSITION

FIGURE 12–4

Figure 12–4: The victim executes a knife kick to the assailant's knee. Note that her hands are up to protect her face, and her non-kicking leg is bent. This supports the kick and will help her to rise to her feet.

ONE KNEE DEFENSE POSITION

FIGURE 12–5

Figure 12–5: From a one-knee position the victim executes a lead-hand fore-fist punch to the groin.

TURRET DEFENSE POSITION

FIGURE 12–6   FIGURE 12–7   FIGURE 12–8

This position gets its name because of the clockwise and counterclockwise movements resembling the turret atop a military tank. The defensive movement is accomplished by pivoting on the buttocks. The direction of movement is achieved by pushing on the ground with your hands. Movement can be as little as a few degrees right or left, or as much as 360 degrees.

Figure 12–6: Lean back and support your weight on your hands. Kick out at the assailant's knees whenever he closes the distance.

Figure 12–7: The assailant begins to circle, and the victim pivots on her buttocks using her hands for momentum. The kicks can be continued.

Figure 12–8: The victim lands a kick to the assailant's knee.

13

Escapes from Holds and Grabs

The element of surprise is a common method employed by an assailant to instill fear in a victim and take immediate control. Many times this is accomplished by seizing the victim in a violent hold or grab. Victims untrained in defensive tactics will react by twisting and turning against the attack, or attempt to dislodge the hands or arms of the attacker by pushing and pulling to no avail. These panic-driven reactions are not only ineffective, they also expend a tremendous amount of energy. This quick loss of energy depletes all the strength and power reserves of the victim in a matter of seconds. When this occurs, breathing becomes labored and difficult, the stress level soars off the chart, and sheer panic sets in. Panic is the number one cause of an unsuccessful defense in a life-threatening encounter.

Advantages of Being Held or Grabbed

When the assailant perpetrates a hold or a grab, there are several advantages that the victim (you) will have over the assailant.

1. The assailant has actually compromised himself by restricting the use of one or both hands.
2. The assailant is expending his own energy through the execution of the hold or grab.
3. The assailant, because of the element of surprise, *expects* the victim to struggle and panic.
4. Any hold or grab can be broken.
5. Relax and evaluate the situation, this only takes a few seconds. *Do not struggle.*
6. *Do not panic!*

The realization of these factors is essential for a safe and successful defense against a hold or grab. What steps can you take against your assailant's hold or grab?

1. Control your breathing to control your panic. Take long, slow, deep breaths.
2. Set your weight if you are standing. Widening your stance and lowering your center-of-balance will accomplish this. When your weight is centered and lowered it is more difficult for the assailant to move you off balance.
3. Use strikes, kicks, or pressure points to escape the hold or grab.

Techniques

The following series of photographs and explanations demonstrate applicable defensive measures against various holds and grabs. The measures shown here employ a variety of techniques including pressure points, kicks and strikes, and takedowns. In real life, you will need to use several techniques to end an attack. Do not rely on a single technique in any self-defense encounter. Always overload on your attacker.

HAND OR WRIST GRAB

FIGURE 13–1

FIGURE 13–2

FIGURE 13–3

Figure 13–1: Set your weight by stepping back, and strike the top of the assailant's hand with the knuckles of your fist.

Figure 13–2: Execute a sidekick to the assailant's knee.

Figure 13–3: Execute a knee-kick to the assailant's head.

If, when you step back to set your weight, your assailant pulls your movement to a halt, *do not* panic. Change your tactic and rush at him with all your force. Drive the hand or forearm of your free arm into his face, neck, or whatever body part is available. You can also drive your head into his face or chest. Use his momentum to your advantage. *Always* give the assailant what he wants.

LAPEL GRAB

FIGURE 13–4

FIGURE 13–5

FIGURE 13–6

Figure 13–4: Step back, setting your weight and unbalancing your attacker. Jump toward the attacker, and with all your body weight deliver an elbow strike to the attacker's forearm.

Figure 13–5: Execute a double palm-heel strike to the attacker's jaw.

Figure 13–6: Execute a low-kick to the attacker's knee.

If the attacker moves and angles his body out of the line of your counter when you jump toward him, *do not* stop your forward momentum. Continue with all your force and unbalance him. Remember, when he is unbalanced he is vulnerable. Use his momentum against him and follow-up with a barrage of techniques and/or a throw or takedown.

FRONT SHOULDER GRAB

FIGURE 13–7

FIGURE 13–8

FIGURE 13–9

FIGURE 13–10

FIGURE 13–11

Figure 13–7 and Figure 13–8: Step back, setting your weight, and raise your arm high above your head.

Figure 13–9: Turn into the grab in the direction of your raised arm. It is important to continue your turn until the attacker releases his grab, or until the attacker is off balance.

Figure 13–10: With the raised arm, deliver a forearm or elbow strike to the attacker's head.

Figure 13–11: Execute a knee-kick to the attacker's knee.

If, when you turn in the direction of your raised arm, your attacker also turns to avoid your counter, immediately turn in the opposite direction, and continue with the same set of counters. Again, give your assailant what he wants.

FRONT ONE-HAND CHOKE

FIGURE 13–12

FIGURE 13–13

FIGURE 13–14

FIGURE 13–15

Figure 13–12: and Figure 13–13: Step back and deliver a double hammer-fist strike to the attacker's wrist.

Figure 13–14: Execute a double spear-hand strike to the attacker's throat.

Figure 13–15: Execute a knee-kick to the attacker's groin.

Again, when you step back, if your attacker tightens his grip and pulls, immediately lunge toward him and drive your forearms down into the area of his elbows. Follow-up by grabbing him by the head and twisting it, taking him to the ground. Once again, you gave him what he wanted.

FRONT TWO-HAND CHOKE

FIGURE 13–16

FIGURE 13–17

FIGURE 13–18

FIGURE 13–19

Figure 13–16: Step back and raise your arm high above your head.

Figure 13–17: Turn into the attacker's grab in the direction of your raised arm.

Figure 13–18: Deliver a hammer-fist strike to the attacker's head.

Figure 13–19: Execute a low-kick to the attacker's calf.

If your attacker impedes your movement by pulling when you step back, his action will cause his elbows to bend. Lunge forward and drive your forearms down into the area of his elbows. Immediately grab his head and deliver a head-thrust to his face.

REAR SHOULDER OR NECK GRAB

FIGURE 13–20

FIGURE 13–21

FIGURE 13–22

FIGURE 13–23

Figure 13–20: Step forward and raise your arm high above your head.

Figure 13–21: Turn 180 degrees in the direction of your raised arm.

Figure 13–22: Deliver an inside forearm strike to the attacker's head.

Figure 13–23: Deliver a knee-kick to the attacker's mid-section.

If, when you turn in the direction of your raised arm your attacker turns also to avoid your counter, immediately turn in the opposite direction, and continue with the same set of counters. Again, give your assailant what he wants.

FRONT BEAR HUG

FIGURE 13–24   FIGURE 13–25   FIGURE 13–26

Figure 13–24: Step back, setting your weight.

Figure 13–25: Deliver simultaneous palm strikes to the attacker's ears.

Figure 13–26: Deliver a knee-kick to the attacker's groin.

If he does not release his grip when you strike your attacker's ears, *do not* panic. Thrust your thumbs into his eyes, and drive his head to the rear. Follow-up with a barrage of kicks to his groin and legs.

REAR BEAR HUG

FIGURE 13–27   FIGURE 13–28   FIGURE 13–29

Figure 13–27: Step to the side to set your weight.

Figure 13–28: Grind and twist the knuckles of your hand onto the top of the attacker's hand.

Figure 13–29: Execute a back-kick to the attacker's knee.

If the action of grinding your knuckles into the top of the attacker's hand does not cause him to release his grip, *do not panic*. With all the speed and strength you can generate, twist your body from side-to-side and execute a continuous series of elbow strikes to his head. When you are free from the hold, *overload* on his legs and knees with a barrage of kicks.

FRONT MID-SECTION HOLD (1)

FIGURE 13–30   FIGURE 13–31   FIGURE 13–32

Figure 13–30: Step back and set your weight.

Figure 13–31: Reach around the attacker's face and grab his chin. With your other hand grab the back of the attacker's head. Twist your arms in the direction of the hand that is holding his jaw and execute a head-twist takedown.

Figure 13–32: Deliver a heel kick to the attacker's head.

If you are unable to grab the attacker's chin and head, alternate your course of action. Drive your thumbs into the attacker's throat and force him back. Execute a series of knee-kicks to his groin and stomach.

FRONT MID-SECTION HOLD (2)

FIGURE 13–33   FIGURE 13–34   FIGURE 13–35

Figure 13–33: Step back and set your weight. Execute a downward elbow strike to the attacker's back between the shoulder blades.

Figure 13–34: Grasp the hand of your elbow-strike arm and push down with all your force. Continue pushing downward and step back, forcing the attacker to the ground.

Figure 13–35: Execute a kick to the attacker's head.

If, when you are pushing down on the attacker's back (Figure 13–34), you cannot step back to get free, *do not panic*. Continue pushing down and go to the ground on your knees. Wrap your arms around the attacker's head, and with your entire force drop down, bringing the attacker's face to the ground.

REAR CHOKE HOLD

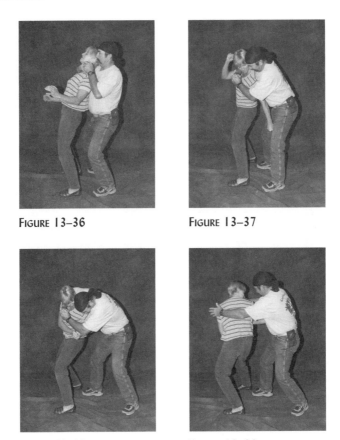

FIGURE 13–36

FIGURE 13–37

FIGURE 13–38

FIGURE 13–39

Figure 13–36: Step to the side and set your weight. Grab the attacking arm and force your chin down into his forearm.

Figure 13–37: Execute a hammer-fist strike to the attacker's groin.

Figure 13–38 and Figure 13–39: Deliver a series of rear elbow strikes to the attacker's mid-section until you are free.

If you are still unable to free yourself, *do not panic*. Again, grab the attacker's arm and continue to twist your head until you are able to bring your mouth in contact anywhere on his arm. Bite the attacker's arm as hard as you can until you are free.

HEADLOCK HOLD

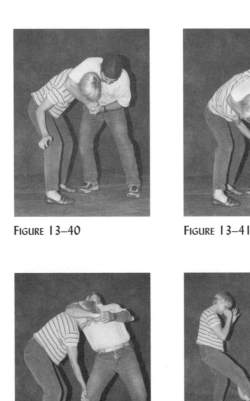

FIGURE 13–40   FIGURE 13–41

FIGURE 13–42   FIGURE 13–43

Figure 13–40: Step to the side and set your weight.

Figure 13–41: Execute a palm-heel strike to his knee with the hand farthest from his body. This is a distraction technique. Follow the distraction immediately with the next move.

Figure 13–42: With your other hand reach up and over the attacker's back and head and dig your fingertips into his eyes. Forcefully pull the attacker's head back and take him to the ground.

Figure 13–43: Disable the attacker with kicks.

If this action does not set you free, *do not panic*. Drive your body into the attacker's leg closest to you and continue to push as you go to the ground.

> **NOTE:** It is not recommended that you attempt to free yourself from a headlock by attempting to lift the attacker off the ground. This action causes the attacker to pull back on your head making you more vulnerable to being choked or having your neck snapped. In addition, many individuals do not posses the required strength to perform such an action.

Never give up through all your attempts to extricate yourself from the assailant's grasp. You will need to dig deep within yourself for that reserve of energy. Control your breathing and focus on the situation. If physical actions fail, attempt dialogue. Play on the assailant's emotions, going to the extreme. It may buy you time and he may just release his grip if he feels he is in control. If he does, you have won this battle, but the war still rages on. Your focus should now be on escape.

Holds and grabs are the most common form of attack. Incarcerated criminals revealed in studies that the reasons they favored grabs and holds were twofold:

1. A physical and emotional shock is thrust upon the victim.
2. They had control over their victims.

Be aware of your surroundings. If there is a glimmer of warning of physical violence, attempt to escape or impede, subdue, and neutralize your attacker before he is able to grab or hold you.

14

Defense Against Punches and Kicks

Everyone has seen his or her share of martial arts and action movies in which the good guy single-handedly, and unarmed, disposes of an army of bad guys. The fight scenes show the combatants engaging each other with series upon series of combinations of punches, kicks, strikes, and blocks. Hands and feet move with lightning speed, parrying and countering. In the end, the good guy dusts himself off and walks off into the sunset. But, that is Hollywood.

Real life is just the opposite. For the most part, physical confrontations involve a push or shove, a grab or hold, or the threat of a weapon. Rarely, will it involve the attacker and victim squaring off, taking up their respective boxer or martial art stance, and putting up their fists to duke it out with one another.

Fighting in a boxing or martial art competition requires rules and, for the most part, some form of protective equipment. Even under these sterile conditions, opponents fail to land blows, block or parry attacks, counterattack, use proper distance and body-and-foot movements. The less experienced the fighters, the more prominent the actions.

The ability to stand toe-to-toe with an opponent and fight, using only body-and-foot techniques, no grabbing, holding, or wrestling, is difficult to say the least, and demanding.

You must have exceptional cardiovascular endurance in order to ward off the stress, and maintain a pace that is equivalent to running numerous wind sprints. You must be in top-notch physical condition, including weight in proportion to height, flexibility, strength, and power. You must be able to concentrate on ignoring the pain associated with the impact of the blows. You must also be able to focus on your opponent and pick up any signs of telegraphing, the unconscious body moves, change in breathing rhythm, or shift in eye movement done before executing a technique. You need to be able to anticipate your opponent's next move. On top of all of that, your techniques must possess speed, power, strength, rhythm, and accuracy.

Real life-threatening fighting requires realistic training. Performing countless repetitions of techniques, with only the air as resistance is a whole lot different from being faced with someone who is trying to take your head and stuff it where you do not want to think about.

Executing endless numbers of techniques in the air is the starting point, and this practice is useful. Repetition builds strength, power, endurance, accuracy, muscle-memory, and speed. For these qualities to grow, each repetition of a specific technique must be performed with attention to detail, full-power, and at a speed that is under control. Speed does not build speed. Speed in training produces sloppy, weak, inaccurate techniques. Long hours of training, accompanied by sweat, patience, and hard work are the keys to proficiency.

It may look impressive to see someone throwing a series of rapid-fire techniques with blinding speed, but in most cases, they are all show and glitz. They lack focus, power, and accuracy. You can throw as many techniques as you like, as fast as you can. But if they cannot land on a vital part of the body with power, accuracy, and penetration to cause blunt-force trauma, they are useless.

You might think that after witnessing the martial arts movies, and martial arts training and competition, that the only techniques are those that are performed high in the air, with large spinning and circular movements. This is a poor representation of the fighting arts. Individuals who are proficient in the skills of hand-to-hand combat would never engage in such antics in a life-threatening self-defense encounter. Their choice of techniques would be linear.

Straight-line techniques are easier to learn and execute. They require less body movements, and therefore, your defense is not open as often, which would leave you vulnerable to a counter. They reach their intended target faster—the shortest distance between two points is a straight line. They are more accurate, deliver more power, and are harder to block than circular techniques.

Circular techniques require more training because they are harder to learn. There are far more elements to comprehend. Do not lift the knee so high that it breaks your balance. Rotate the hip and pivot on the ball of the foot. These are just two of many things you must be aware during training. Swinging an arm or leg in a wide arc exposes too many body parts to the opponent. In a real-life self-defense situation, you also run the risk of striking a variety of inanimate objects that are within the immediate area, such as furniture, light posts, trees, automobiles, and other individuals. Circular techniques are adequate if they are short-range.

Just because you practice a martial art does not mean that your techniques are applicable for self-defense, or that you are a fighter. No matter what type of technique you prefer, to be proficient for fighting requires a training program that is without showmanship and glitz, is on-going, and realistic. My students spend hours, upon hours, upon hours standing toe-to-toe engaging in fighting exercises where only punches, strikes, kicks, and blocks are permitted. They must also use proper distance, and body-and-foot movements. This toe-to-toe form of fighting is difficult to master and rarely practiced in today's martial art schools. It requires years of training and is not for everyone.

The following photographs demonstrate blocking, countering, distancing, and body-and-foot movement—all essential elements for toe-to-toe fighting.

FRONT JAB

FIGURE 14–1   FIGURE 14–2   FIGURE 14–3

Figure 14–1: Step to the outside of the punching arm and deflect the punch with your rearward arm.

Figure 14–2: Slide your arm up and over the punching arm and strike the attacker's head with your forearm.

Figure 14–3: Execute a back-to-back throw.

HOOK PUNCH

FIGURE 14–4   FIGURE 14–5

FIGURE 14–6   FIGURE 14–7

Figure 14–4: Block the inside of the punching arm with your lead arm.

Figure 14–5 and Figure 14–6: Execute a series of palm-heel strikes to the attacker's jaw.

Figure 14–7: Execute a knee kick to the attacker's groin.

ONE-TWO PUNCH

FIGURE 14–8   FIGURE 14–9   FIGURE 14–10

FIGURE 14–11   FIGURE 14–12

Figure 14–8: Execute an open-hand block to the attacking arm.

Figure 14–9: With your same hand, continue to move your arm across your opponent and block his next punch.

Figure 14–10 through Figure 14–12: Deliver a series of hammer-fist strikes to the attacker's head.

FRONT KICK (1)

FIGURE 14–13   FIGURE 14–14   FIGURE 14–15

Figure 14–13: Step to the outside to avoid the kicking leg.

Figure 14–14: Execute a hammer-fist strike to the assailant's back.

Figure 14–15: Grab the assailant's head and pull backward.

FIGURE 14–16   FIGURE 14–17

Figure 14–16: Continue to pull the assailant's head back and down, taking him to the ground.

Figure 14–17: Once he is down, execute a kick to the assailant's head.

FRONT KICK (2)

FIGURE 14–18   FIGURE 14–19   FIGURE 14–20

Figure 14–18: Step to the outside to avoid the kicking leg.

Figure 14–19: Grasp the attacker's kicking leg and begin to lift.

Figure 14–20: Execute a low-kick to the attacker's support leg and throw him to the ground.

Low Kick

FIGURE 14–21   FIGURE 14–22   FIGURE 14–23

Figure 14–21: Block the attacking leg with your shin. This may hurt if your legs are not conditioned, but it is better than having your leg kicked out from under you.

Figure 14–22: Execute a palm-heel strike to the attacker's face area.

Figure 14–23: Execute a kick to the attacker's groin.

The photographs and accompanying text in this book make self-defense look easy. These photographs were taken in a sterile setting, and my student, Danny, and I were not trying to take one another's head off. At times it may have appeared to those watching that it was escalating to that stage. This toe-to-toe, close-quarter fighting is not easy. The amount of training required to become proficient in these techniques is too long for most individuals to endure. Practice, practice, practice, and then practice some more. Only then will you understand your limitations.

15

Unique Situations

The ability to defend oneself is not limited to open areas, such as on the street, where your maneuvering, distancing, and counter-attacks are unrestricted. Assailants select not only their victims, but the location that will present them with the best opportunity to carry out their acts. Many acts of aggression will take place in confined and limited spaces. The interior of a vehicle, or home, are favorite venues of violent acts. The invader knows that such locations confine the victim, limit the victim's course of action, and provide the element of surprise.

The average citizen feels secure once inside the comfortable surroundings of a vehicle, or home, or in public areas, such as on a bus or in a movie theater. Again, the assailant who does his homework knows this and uses it to his advantage. Victims of attacks in such settings are always surprised to be attacked in such seemingly secure and comfortable areas.

Home invasion and car-jacking (crime against person abducted in his or her own vehicle) are occurrences that are still somewhat new and therefore unexpected. However, these two criminal acts are on the rise and the accompanying violence can be the most horrendous a victim might ever experience. Home invasions and car-jackings carry an additional element of physical and emotional abuse: one's private space is violated and proven not to be safe. The physical scars may heal, but the mental scars last a lifetime. The violent physical assault associated with these two crimes is so traumatic that most victims are left disabled, or do not survive the attack.

If you are attacked while inside your vehicle *never* drive off under the command of the attacker, and *never* allow the attacker to drive off while you are in the car. You must use every resource available to you; this includes crashing your vehicle to facilitate your escape.

Personal protection is the ability to defend under all circumstances. This includes riding on a bus or subway, in your own vehicle, or any other confined spaces. The techniques practiced from a standing, well-balanced position should be applicable in all self-defense scenarios, whether you are in a prone, supine, or a seated position. It is essential that your self-defense training address all such situations. Following are some specific scenarios with tips on how to escape.

Attacks in Confined Spaces

Self-defense in confined spaces is close-quarter fighting. In this environment short-range distance is a given, and body-and-foot movement is restricted. Techniques that produce a lot of power, such as elbow strikes, knee kicks, and head strikes, are the most applicable. Rolling and avoidance techniques are also applicable. The key—don't panic.

WHEN YOU ARE ATTACKED IN BED

1. Do not panic and attempt to pull or push the attacker free. This will only expend needed energy.
2. Raise your arms toward the sky.
3. Rock side-to-side and strike your arms against the arms of the attacker. He is on the same unstable base as you are and will become unbalanced from your attacks.
4. Dig your thumbs or fingertips into the eyes or neck of the attacker.
5. Execute a series of elbow strikes to the face and head of the attacker until he is stunned. Free yourself, flee to a nearby residence, and call 911.

Here's one scenario involving someone being attacked in a bed.

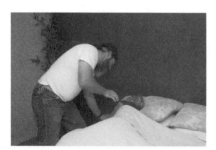

FIGURE 15–1

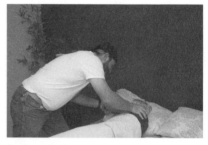

FIGURE 15–2

FIGURE 15–3

FIGURE 15–4

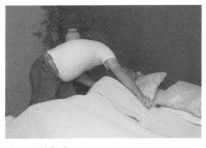

FIGURE 15–5

FIGURE 15–6

FIGURE 15–7

FIGURE 15–8

Figure 15–1: Assailant approaches a sleeping victim.

Figure 15–2: Assailant grabs the victim.

Figure 15–3: Victim executes a palm heel strike to the assailant's jaw. Note that she has maintained her presence of mind and has not panicked.

Figure 15–4: Using the same arm, the victim follows up with an elbow strike to the head.

Figure 15–5: Victim rolls into the assailant's arm in order to unbalance him.

Figure 15–6: Victim reverses her direction and rolls against his opposite arm.

Figure 15–7: Victim gouges the assailant's eyes with her thumbs.

Figure 15–8: Victim continues to attack his eyes with one hand. With the other arm she executes an elbow strike to the throat.

Attacks in Vehicles

Car-jacking, where the assailant attacks you in your own vehicle, usually is nothing more than a kidnapping. Most car-jackings include homicides. If an assailant only wanted your money, he would reach in and take it. No matter how much you are threatened, *never* give in to the assailant's demands and drive away. You must use everything within your power to escape.

WHEN YOU ARE ATTACKED IN A CAR (FROM THE REAR)

FIGURE 15–9

FIGURE 15–10

FIGURE 15–11

Figure 15–9: Victim attacked by an assailant who was hiding in the rear seat area of her vehicle.

Figure 15–10: Using the steering wheel for leverage, the victim pulls violently while lunging her body forward to break free from the hold. If your lunge forward does not free you from the assailant's hold, immediately lunge backward and then forward. Continue this until you have broken free or are in a position where you can bite any portion of the assailant's arm or hand. If your pulling and pushing has not broken the assailant's grasp, nor presented the opportunity to bite him, you must resort to another tactic. Release your grip on the wheel, dig and tear at your attacker's hand with your fingernails. If possible, sound the horn. If all attempts to break free from his grasp fail, place the vehicle in gear for whatever direction of travel is open, floor the accelerator and drive—crash the vehicle.

Figure 15–11: The victim is fleeing the vehicle after breaking free from her attacker. Escape from the vehicle to a safe location and call 911.

CAR-JACKING (ATTEMPT TO PULL YOU OUT OF THE CAR, OR ABDUCTION)

FIGURE 15-12

FIGURE 15-13

FIGURE 15-14

FIGURE 15-15

FIGURE 15-16

FIGURE 15-17

Figure 15–12: Assailant yanks open the vehicle door.

Figure 15–13: Victim dives across the seat and grabs the door-handle or seat to keep from being extracted.

Figure 15–14: Victim kicks the assailant's groin. Your choice of targets is whatever is available and closest to you.

Figure 15–15: Victim blitzes with a continuous barrage of kicks aimed at the attacker.

Figure 15–16: Victim opens the passenger side door and dives out of the vehicle.

Figure 15–17: Victim flees to a safe location and calls 911.

Attacks in Confined Spaces

Several of our day-to-day activities place us in confined spaces, thus restricting movement and ease of escape. One of the most common activities, and one that presents numerous obstacles for movement, is dining in a restaurant. While seated, the use of your legs is all but non-existent due to the confinement of the table. On the table, however, there may be a tablecloth, and there will be utensils, plates, glasses, salt and pepper shakers, and other condiments. There may be even a candle or a flower arrangement. In addition to all this, there will be food and beverages.

Linear Device is a term used by the military and law enforcement tactical groups to describe certain conveyances, such as planes, trains, and buses. An assault on such a conveyance is the most dangerous scenario these tactical groups face. It is also one of the most dangerous areas to be in or to defend. Confined, restricted movement is paramount, and avenues of escape are limited or non-existent.

Places and conveyances where we conduct day-to-day activities are not immune from violence, but they do present situations of self-defense. Confined spaces, such as theaters, restaurants, and conveyances are not conducive arenas if you are attacked. Some are noisy, while some are quiet. Some are dark, while others are too well lit. Some have structural designs unfavorable to free movement. If you find yourself in such a situation your first thought should be to use as defensive instruments, whatever objects or implements are readily available. Because it is likely you will be seated, your second thought should be to remain seated, if possible, throughout the encounter. Seated, you are already in a strong, stable position. Your center-of-gravity is low, making it difficult for your attacker to lift you. In addition, remaining seated makes your attacker come to you. In order to do this he will have to bend and lean down. He is then unbalanced and vulnerable, exactly where you want him. If you do find yourself on your feet, you will need to resort to close-quarter techniques (no wide, circular, or arching moves) that use your head, hands, forearms, and elbows. It will be almost impossible to use your legs for kicking purposes.

The following are depictions of seated defensive measures. They can be employed in any of the environments mentioned above.

SEATED ATTACK FROM THE FRONT

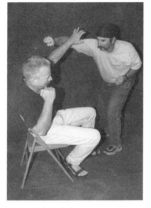 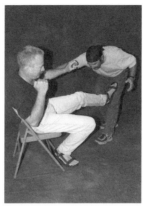 

FIGURE 15–18   FIGURE 15–19   FIGURE 15–20

Figure 15–18: Do not panic and attempt to stand up. Block the strike with your arm.
Figure 15–18: Execute a kick to the attacker's knee.
Figure 15–20: Punch the attacker's neck or head.

SEATED ATTACK FROM THE SIDE (1)

  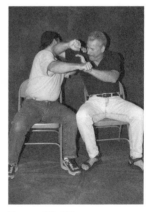

FIGURE 15–21   FIGURE 15–22   FIGURE 15–23

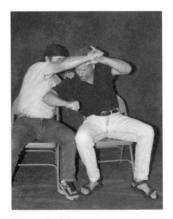

FIGURE 5–24

FIGURE 5–25

Figure 15–21: Attacker grabs you and attempts to strike or pull you with his opposite hand.

Figure 15–22: Block your attacker's second advance with your farthest arm and execute an elbow strike to his head with your opposite arm..

Figure 15–23: Execute a series of elbow strikes to the attacker's face and chest area. With your free hand, grab your opponent's wrist.

Figure 15–24: Turn toward the attacker and drive your elbow or fist into his groin.

SEATED ATTACK FROM THE SIDE (2)

FIGURE 5–26

FIGURE 5–27

FIGURE 5–28

FIGURE 5–29

Figure 15–25: The attacker places his arm around you in an attempt to remove you from your seat. Drive a hammer fist strike into the groin of the attacker.

Figure 15–26: Grab the attacker by the chin and back of head and throw him to the ground.

Figure 15–27: Execute a series of kicks to the attacker.

Crowded Areas

The preceding photographs illustrating seated defense measures do not adequately portray real-life conditions. In real life, the locations and conveyances mentioned are open to the public and most likely will be crowded with other people.

Crowds present problems at the sites of physical confrontations between two or more individuals. If alcohol is present, the problems are worsened several times over. The following are some of the more common problems associated with crowds.

- The more people present, the fewer avenues of escape will you have. The crowd may be so large that you have no avenue of escape.
- Crowds restrict your movements and limit your choice of techniques.
- Crowds are inclined to take sides, and then begin to cheer on and instigate their favorite. This will give your attacker an extra boost of confidence. Moreover, some in the crowd may join with your attacker and converge on you.

If you find yourself in a confrontation within a crowd, speak to your aggressor, and try not to resort to physical measures. Make every attempt to flee the area.

Two of our most popular public venues today are the epitome of confined spaces: movie theaters and airplanes. Both present unique problems when it comes to physical conflicts requiring self-defense.

In movie theaters, in addition to restricted movement in any direction, the floors are constructed on an angle, and they are dark. These last two items are detrimental to the body's mechanics and senses. However, you just may be able to use them to your advantage.

In the dark, it becomes easier to conceal yourself, which strengthens your chances of escape. Also, the time to react to a blow may be shortened because you may not see it coming until it is on top of you. Your attacker will not see it coming either; use this to your advantage.

Fighting on a sloped floor destroys your balance and center of gravity. Fighting uphill reduces the effectiveness of your techniques. In this position, however, leverage and motion are on your side. Use throws and takedowns. When fighting downhill, it is very difficult to control your forward momentum. A commercial airliner is the definitive confined space. There are no avenues of escape. Seatbacks are high and ceiling is low, which makes climbing over seats difficult. Because there are so many of them, the seats are a continuous obstacle course. The occupants of the seats restrict your lateral movements. Aisles are narrow, limiting your direction of movement to forward and backward, which limits your choice of techniques. Circular techniques are useless, for you have no room to execute them. Close-range, straight-line techniques using your elbows, knees, and head are your best options.

You should also attempt to use the everyday items at your disposal. The interior of a commercial airliner contains a myriad of everyday items that can be used for self-defense. There are books, magazines, laptop computers, cell phones, portable CD players, cameras, pens and pencils, eyeglasses, luggage, clothing, the list is endless. You can also remove the seat cushion, place your arm through the straps on the underside, and use it as a shield, or to smash into someone. The only limits are your imagination.

Defending yourself in a confined space is a worst-case scenario. Circular techniques, distancing, body-and-foot movement, throws and takedowns, ground avoidance rolls, escape attempts, just about everything in your self-defense repertoire is either restricted or totally useless. Because of the limited resources, you must utilize whatever items you can lay your hands on and whatever windows of opportunity are presented to you. Self-defense in confined spaces requires that you act, rather than react.

I have instructed thousands of people, from all walks of life, from all over the world on the subject of self-defense. Over the years, I have received telephone calls, letters, e-mail messages, and even telegraphs from many individuals thanking me for what I taught them—for, as they related, the knowledge saved their lives. This may sound unbelievable that so many individuals were put in situations that required defense against physical violence. If you consider the number of people I have instructed, the number of those involved in a real-life self-defense situation is less than two percent. In addition, except for two of these individuals, the encounters were the result of their occupation, and not their personal lives.

I am grateful that the self-defense instruction these individuals received from me proved beneficial.

If only one individual avoids physical violence after having read this book, I have done my job and I will be happy.

What would make me even happier is for everyone who reads this book never to be put in a situation in which they must protect themselves or others from physical harm using self-defense techniques.

References

Anderson, D. "The Aggregate Burden of Crime," *Journal of Law and Economics*, 42: 611-42 (1999).

Federal Bureau of Investigation, *Uniform Crime Report*. Washington, D.C.: 2000.

Koppel, Herbert. 1987. *Lifetime Likelihood of Victimization*. Prepared by the U.S. Department of Justice, Bureau of Justice Statistics. Washington, D.C.

About the Author

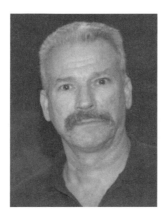

Mr. Lorden is a branch chief-instructor for the Kyokushin Karate Organization of Tokyo, Japan. His association and experience in karate exceeds forty years. In addition to his karate experience, he holds certifications in defensive tactics from the FBI and the U.S. Military. He has trained more than two thousand law enforcement personnel, from agencies throughout the country, in defensive tactics. He has also trained numerous military personnel including U.S. Army Special Forces and British SAS. His certified instructor status includes firearms, high-risk tactical operations, rappelling, PR-24 baton, ASP baton, physical fitness specialist, as well as other specialized areas of high-risk special operations. Mr. Lorden is a court-certified expert in defensive tactics, chemical agents, and high-risk tactical operations. He holds a B.S. in business management. He is a graduate of the ISC Division of Wellness (Fitness Specialist-Physical Wellness Planner). Mr. Lorden is the author of several articles and newsletters, as well as a book on law enforcement defensive tactics. He is a full-time writer, as well as a Kyokushin Karate instructor. He currently resides in Colorado Springs, Colorado with his wife, Jennifer, where they own and operate their Kyokushin Dojo.